YOUTH
BIBLE STUDY
NOTEBOOK

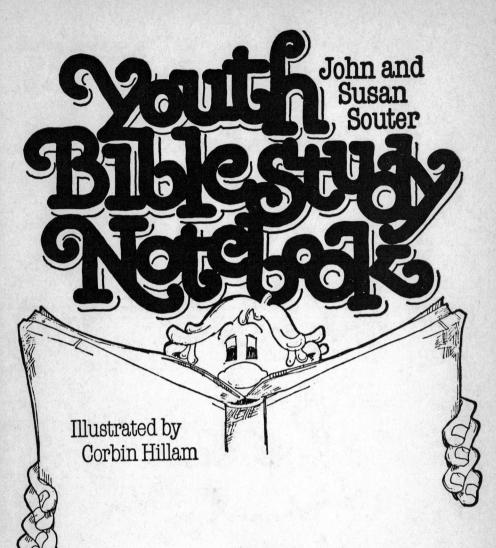

Youth Bible Study Notebook

John and
Susan
Souter

Illustrated by
Corbin Hillam

Tyndale House
Publishers, Inc.
Wheaton, Illinois

CON

Seventh printing, September 1981

Youth Bible Study Notebook
ISBN 0–8423–8790–0, paper.
Copyright © 1977 by John C. Souter.

TENTS

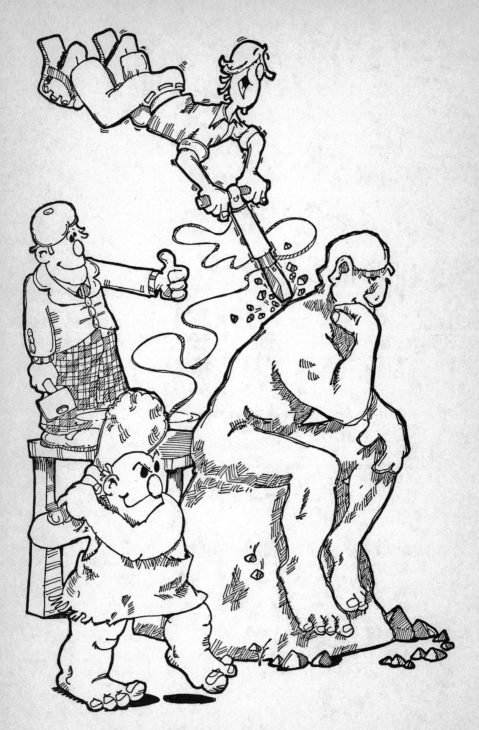

1 THAT OLD BOOK?

Imagine several sculptors living at different times of history and in different lands. Every artist creates a large piece of a statue. Each works by himself. After the years pass, the pieces are collected and put together. To everyone's surprise, they fit together perfectly and make a beautiful work of art.

This is what happened with the Bible. It was written by at least thirty-seven authors, in two languages, over a period of about 2,000 years. Yet, its sixty-six books fit together beautifully. Who but God could have done this?

"Now wait a minute," you say, "I've tried to read the Bible and it just doesn't make sense. I could never get past all those 'begats.'"

Is this your experience? Is the Bible just an old book to you? The Youth Bible Study Notebook will show you how to get exciting truths out of God's Word.

First, you must know that reading the Bible from the front to the back is like reading a dictionary from A to Z. Parts will be interesting but the Bible wasn't really meant to be read that way. This notebook will show you how to study the Bible piece by piece.

Second, if the Bible seems old and stale, you should try a more contemporary translation. The Bible is not the King James Version (a translation finished in 1611). The Bible was written originally in Hebrew and Greek, and there are many English translations (including the King James) from which to choose. The Way (youth edition of The Living Bible) is a modern paraphrase of the Bible that is as easy to read as a newspaper, and would undoubtedly be a big help in your study.

2
WHY STUDY THE BIBLE?

Would you like to be wiser than your enemies? Would you like to be wiser than your teachers? Would you like everything you do to be blessed by God?

Of course you would. Well, God promises to make you wise if you study and love His Book. If you study it faithfully, He will enrich your life. (See Psalm 119:98, 99; James 1:25.)

The Bible calls itself a two-edged sword that can cut into your thoughts and desires (Hebrews 4:12). When you look into God's Word, you will discover all kinds of things—about yourself. The Bible will show you how to live. It will reveal things that must change in your life, and tell you what God wants you to do.

When you like someone, you try to spend time with him or her, don't you? (I sure hope you do!) Well, if you really love God, you'll want to spend time studying His words.

The Bible is part of a love affair between God and His people. Read Psalm 119. David, the king who wrote it, was obviously in love with God. He couldn't stop thinking about God. Because David loved God so much, he couldn't stay away from His laws.

Do you love God that much? Before long God will begin to bless your life. The Bible is the greatest book ever written. It will make you a happy Christian when you dig deeply into its pages.

Gettin' the Habit. How often do you study your Bible? Every day? Every other day? Once a week? Or maybe just once in a while? If you really love God, you will want to spend lots of time in His Book learning how to be a better Christian.

It really is hard to spend time in God's book, isn't it? Every time you open it up, for some reason you get sidetracked and the next thing you know you haven't looked in the Bible for weeks.

I have a suggestion. Right now, promise God you will spend <u>at least</u> five minutes in the Bible <u>every</u> day for the next week. You know how you hate to have someone make a promise and then not keep it! When you make your promise to God, you will want to work hard to come through. Thirty-five minutes of study a week is not too much to ask of yourself. Make that promise now.

Later, when you see how that promise will change your attitude toward the Bible, you'll want to make that promise again and again. Next time, give God five minutes a day for a whole month. The Logbook will let you know how you're doing.

Secrets for Success. If you set a time and a place to study, it will be easier to stick to your Bible study time—so set a definite time and place. When will you study?_____
Where will you study?_____

You will not be able to answer all the questions in this notebook. Because the questions are general, they will not all apply to every Bible passage. If one of the questions doesn't fit the passage you are studying, write "NA" for "no answer" and move on.

You will have to look closely at the passage and do some thinking to get good ansrs.

To be a successful Bible student, you must learn to

see what's in a passage. You may have to read the passage more than once. If you look carefully, you'll see things other people miss.

The main reason you study the Bible is to learn what God wants you to be. Don't ever forget to apply God's words to your life. Always look at the Bible expecting God to give something you can use. Always ask Him to show you new truth.

What's in the Bible? Some people would have to say, "Two bookmarks, three pressed flowers, and a two-year-old church bulletin." Many know what they've put in their Bibles, but not what God has put there.

The Bible is not only one book; it is a library of sixty-six different books. Thirty-nine of the books are in the Old Testament, which was written before the birth of Jesus Christ. The other twenty-seven books are in the New Testament, written by those who lived during Christ's lifetime here on earth. Each of these books was written for a different reason. To be able to understand what's in each of them, read about the following groups.

History. The history books in Scripture tell about the men and women who lived during Bible times. In the Old Testament, the beginning of the world is described along with man's first fall into sin. Later books describe the founding of Israel as a nation and all the problems she faced over the years.

In the New Testament the history books tell of Jesus' life and death. They reveal how He rose from the dead, then inspired His followers to change the world.

The books of history are:

The Law. Mixed into the history section of the Old Testament are four books which contain the moral and legal laws of Israel. These laws in some ways resemble the laws of the land in which we live, but they were given by God to His people centuries ago. They reveal God's standards. These laws are found in:

Poetry. Five books in the Old Testament are poetry literature. The book of Psalms is a collection of 150 songs written by King David and a few others. Proverbs is a collection of wise sayings written by Solomon. The poetry books are:

Prophecy. Found mostly in the Old Testament, the prophecy books predict the future of Israel and the world. They announced that Christ was going to come and die for the sins of the world. They also predicted He would come again. The prophecy books are:

Jesus' Teachings. Mixed into the four history books which tell of Christ's earthly life and death are the teachings of Jesus. As God's Son, Jesus was the greatest teacher the world has ever known and His lessons are full of divine truth. The books which contain these teachings are:

The Letters. Most of the New Testament books are letters (sometimes called epistles). These letters were written by several early Christians to people and churches who had needs. They explain what Christianity is all about. These books are:

The fourteen Bible study methods in this notebook will show you how to study every book in the Bible, and how to use those methods.

There are fourteen different methods of Bible study in this notebook. Each method is designed for a different type of Bible passage. Here is a brief description of each of these Bible study tools and an explanation of how to use them.

The Short Methods (5 to 10 minutes each)

<u>Dig In.</u> What is it?—"Dig In" will show you how to look deeply into a few Bible verses.

How to begin—Select a verse or verses to study. Look up that passage and answer the two questions about it.

<u>Wise Up.</u> What is it?—"Wise Up" closely examines the wisdom contained in the book of Proverbs.

How to begin—Almost every Proverb contains a contrast between good and evil or between wisdom and foolishness. Choose a Proverb and study what wise people do and don't do.

<u>Sing Along.</u> What is it?—"Sing Along" takes a look at the book of Psalms.

How to begin—Although the Psalms were once songs, don't expect them to rhyme like modern-day tunes. Quickly read the Psalm you select, then answer the "Sing Along" questions.

<u>The Navigator.</u> What is it?—"The Navigator" will help you work your way through the prophecy books. It is a survey that shows what these books contain.

How to begin—Select a prophecy book to study. In just a few words, write down what each paragraph or chapter says in the space provided. On the left, record the verses found in the passage you looked at. On the right, put a "P" every time a paragraph predicts something.

The Surveyor. What is it?—"The Surveyor" will show you how to take a quick look at the different Bible books. "Surveyor" is like "Navigator," but it is used on books which are not prophecy books.

How to begin—Select a non-prophecy book to study. Write down, in a few words, what each paragraph or chapter says in the space provided. On the left, write the verse references of the paragraph you just read. (For example: chapter one, verses 3 to 9 would be shown: 1:3-9.)

The Watchman. What is it?—"The Watchman" helps you look at longer Bible passages, and reminds you to think about one or two verses throughout your day.

How to begin—Choose a Bible passage. Read it carefully, then answer the questions. Look for one verse which you want to think about all day long.

The Long Methods (15 to 20 minutes)

Manhunt. What is it?—"Manhunt" is a search for the facts about the life of a Bible character.

How to begin—Select a Bible character. You will probably have to skip around the Bible to read the passages which tell of his or her life. Several characters have been selected for you to study. For each of them a number of passages are given. When you have read the material, answer the questions.

Day in Court. What is it?—"Day in Court" is an examination of the rules and regulations which God gave the Israelites.

How to begin—Choose a law and look it up. If the law has been done away in some other part of the Bible, that reference will be given too. After you read about the law, answer the questions.

<u>Get That Story.</u> What is it?—A news reporter tries to get all the facts about an event. "Get That Story" asks the five basic questions every newspaper reporter must ask: who, when, where, what, and why.

How to begin—Select a history passage to study. Read the passage carefully, looking for the answers to the five basic questions. Few historical passages will contain answers to all of the questions, so answer the ones that you can.

<u>The Postal Inspector.</u> What is it?—"Postal Inspector" takes a deeper look at small sections of New Testament letters (or epistles).

How to begin—Choose a passage and read it carefully. Answer the questions after you know what the passage is saying.

<u>The Forecaster.</u> What is it?—"Forecaster" takes you up in the air so that you can study the future. With this method you take a closer look at a prophecy passage.

How to begin—Read the passage you select. (If it has been fulfilled somewhere else in the Bible, that passage will be given too.) Answer the questions after looking at the Scripture carefully.

<u>The University.</u> What is it?—"The University" takes a look at the teachings of Jesus Christ, the Master Teacher.

How to begin—Carefully read the lesson given by Jesus that you select. Then begin to answer the questions. Try to understand the main thing Christ is trying to teach.

<u>Story Time.</u> What is it?—"Story Time" takes a close view of the parables or stories of Jesus.

How to begin—Carefully read the story you select,

then begin to answer the questions. Make certain you understand the meaning of the story.

The Detective (20 to 30 min.). What is it?—"The Detective" searches to find all the facts about a Bible book, its author, and its content.

How to begin—Choose a Bible book. Many of "The Detective" questions can usually be answered from the verses at the beginning and end of the book. However, you should read through the complete book at one sitting so that you can tell what the book is about.

Logbook. What is it?—The "Logbook" is a record of your daily Bible study time. It will show you how often you are getting into the Word of God.

How to begin—Each day after you have studied God's Word, write down the method you used on the blank opposite the day's date.

Choose Your Own Passage. Before each of the methods in this notebook, you will find carefully selected Bible passages for you to study. However, if you want to select your own passages to study, using the methods, you can do so. Just make sure you choose the right type of method for the Bible passage you select. Here is a guide to help you.

The Type of Passage	The Methods You Can Use
HISTORY	The Surveyor
	The Watchman
	Manhunt
	Get That Story
	The Detective
LAW	The Surveyor
	The Watchman
	Day in Court
	The Detective
POETRY	Dig In
	Wise Up
	Sing Along
	The Watchman
	The Detective
PROPHECY	The Navigator
	The Watchman
	Forecaster
	The Detective
JESUS' TEACHINGS	Dig In
	The Surveyor
	The Watchman
	The University
	Story Time
	The Detective
THE LETTERS	Dig In
	The Surveyor
	The Watchman
	The Postal Inspector
	The Detective

DIG IN!

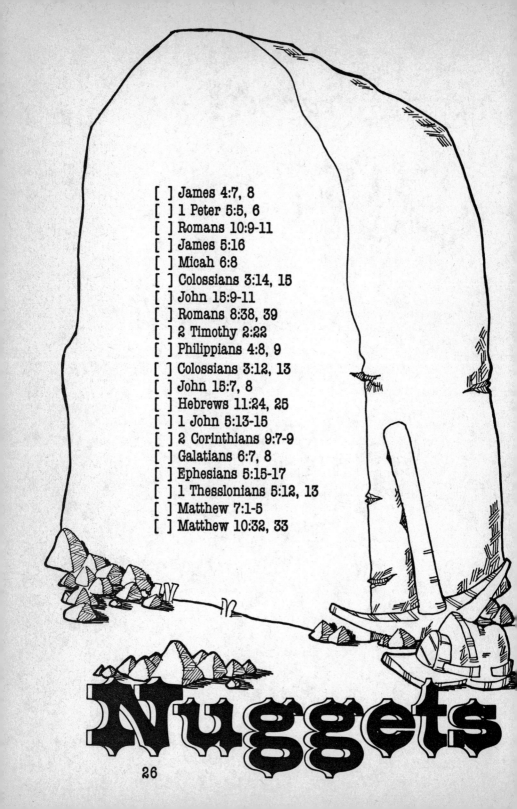

[ ] James 4:7, 8
[ ] 1 Peter 5:5, 6
[ ] Romans 10:9-11
[ ] James 5:16
[ ] Micah 6:8
[ ] Colossians 3:14, 15
[ ] John 15:9-11
[ ] Romans 8:38, 39
[ ] 2 Timothy 2:22
[ ] Philippians 4:8, 9
[ ] Colossians 3:12, 13
[ ] John 15:7, 8
[ ] Hebrews 11:24, 25
[ ] 1 John 5:13-15
[ ] 2 Corinthians 9:7-9
[ ] Galatians 6:7, 8
[ ] Ephesians 5:15-17
[ ] 1 Thesslonians 5:12, 13
[ ] Matthew 7:1-5
[ ] Matthew 10:32, 33

Nuggets

5 to 10 minutes.   Date _____

Verses _____

1. What does this verse say (in my own words)? _____

_____

_____

_____

_____

2. What promises are given? _____

_____

_____

_____

_____

_____

_____

_____

5 to 10 minutes.   Date _____

Verses _____

1. What does this verse say (in my own words)? _____

_____

_____

_____

2. What promises are given? _____

_____

_____

_____

_____

_____ 27

5 to 10 minutes.   Date_____

Verses_____

1. What does this verse say (in my own words)?_____

_____

_____

_____

_____

2. What promises are given?_____

_____

_____

_____

_____

_____

5 to 10 minutes.   Date_____

Verses_____

1. What does this verse say (in my own words)?_____

_____

_____

_____

2. What promises are given?_____

_____

_____

_____

_____

_____

_____

28

5 to 10 minutes.   Date _____

Verses _____

1. What does this verse say (in my own words)? _____
_____
_____
_____
_____

2. What promises are given? _____
_____
_____
_____
_____
_____
_____

5 to 10 minutes.   Date _____

Verses _____

1. What does this verse say (in my own words)? _____
_____
_____
_____

2. What promises are given? _____
_____
_____
_____
_____

5 to 10 minutes.   Date_____

Verses_____

1. What does this verse say (in my own words)?_____

_____ _____

_____

_____

_____

2. What promises are given?_____

_____

_____

_____

_____

_____

_____

5 to 10 minutes.   Date_____

Verses_____

1. What does this verse say (in my own words)?_____

_____

_____

_____

_____

2. What promises are given?_____

_____

_____

_____

_____

_____

_____

_____

5 to 10 minutes.   Date _____

Verses _____

1. What does this verse say (in my own words)? _____

_____

_____

_____

_____

2. What promises are given? _____

_____

_____

_____

_____

_____

_____

5 to 10 minutes.   Date _____

Verses _____

1. What does this verse say (in my own words)? _____

_____

_____

_____

_____

2. What promises are given? _____

_____

_____

_____

_____

_____

5 to 10 minutes.   Date_____

Verses_____

1. What does this verse say (in my own words)?_____

_____

_____

_____

_____

2. What promises are given?_____

_____

_____

_____

_____

_____

5 to 10 minutes.   Date_____

Verses_____

1. What does this verse say (in my own words)?_____

_____

_____

_____

_____

2. What promises are given?_____

_____

_____

_____

_____

_____

5 to 10 minutes.   Date _____

Verses _____

1. What does this verse say (in my own words)? _____

_____

_____

_____

_____

2. What promises are given? _____

_____

_____

_____

_____

_____

5 to 10 minutes.   Date _____

Verses _____

1. What does this verse say (in my own words)? _____

_____

_____

_____

_____

2. What promises are given? _____

_____

_____

_____

_____

_____ 33

5 to 10 minutes.   Date_____

Verses_____

1. What does this verse say (in my own words)?_____

_____

_____

_____

_____

_____

2. What promises are given?_____

_____

_____

_____

_____

_____

_____

_____

5 to 10 minutes.   Date_____

Verses_____

1. What does this verse say (in my own words)?_____

_____

_____

_____

_____

2. What promises are given?_____

_____

_____

_____

_____

_____

_____

_____

5 to 10 minutes. Date _____

Verses _____

1. What does this verse say (in my own words)? _____

_____

_____

_____

_____

2. What promises are given? _____

_____

_____

_____

_____

_____

_____

_____

5 to 10 minutes. Date _____

Verses _____

1. What does this verse say (in my own words)? _____

_____

_____

_____

_____

2. What promises are given? _____

_____

_____

_____

_____

5 to 10 minutes.   Date_____

Verses_____

1. What does this verse say (in my own words)?_____

_____

_____

_____

_____

2. What promises are given?_____

_____

_____

_____

_____

_____

5 to 10 minutes.   Date_____

Verses_____

1. What does this verse say (in my own words)?_____

_____

_____

_____

_____

2. What promises are given?_____

_____

_____

_____

_____

_____

_____

_____

WISE UP

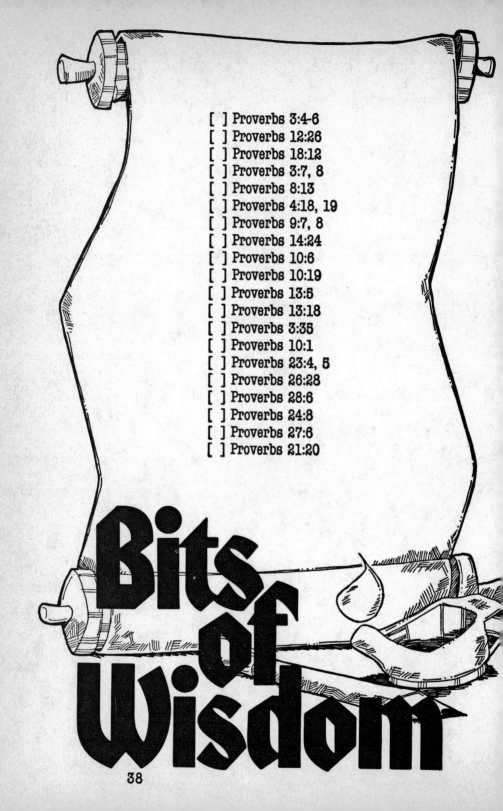

[ ] Proverbs 3:4-6
[ ] Proverbs 12:26
[ ] Proverbs 18:12
[ ] Proverbs 3:7, 8
[ ] Proverbs 8:13
[ ] Proverbs 4:18, 19
[ ] Proverbs 9:7, 8
[ ] Proverbs 14:24
[ ] Proverbs 10:6
[ ] Proverbs 10:19
[ ] Proverbs 13:5
[ ] Proverbs 13:18
[ ] Proverbs 3:35
[ ] Proverbs 10:1
[ ] Proverbs 23:4, 5
[ ] Proverbs 26:28
[ ] Proverbs 28:6
[ ] Proverbs 24:8
[ ] Proverbs 27:6
[ ] Proverbs 21:20

Bits of Wisdom

5 to 10 minutes.   Date _____

Proverb reference _____

1. What good traits (qualities) are given? _____

_____

_____

2. What bad traits (qualities) are given?_____

_____

_____

3. What does this proverb teach me? _____

_____

_____

_____

_____

5 to 10 minutes.   Date _____

Proverb reference _____

1. What good traits (qualities) are given? _____

_____

_____

2. What bad traits (qualities) are given?_____

_____

_____

3. What does this proverb teach me? _____

_____

_____

_____

_____

WISE UP

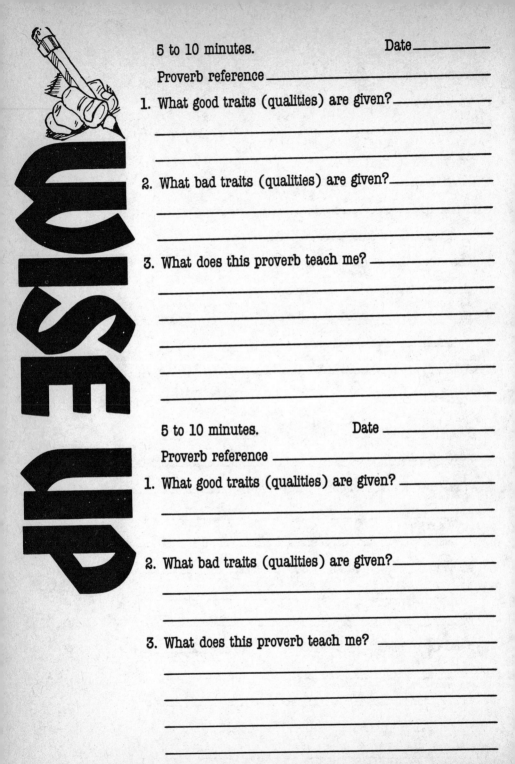

5 to 10 minutes.   Date_____

Proverb reference _____

1. What good traits (qualities) are given?_____
   _____
   _____

2. What bad traits (qualities) are given?_____
   _____
   _____

3. What does this proverb teach me? _____
   _____
   _____
   _____
   _____
   _____

5 to 10 minutes.   Date _____

Proverb reference _____

1. What good traits (qualities) are given? _____
   _____
   _____

2. What bad traits (qualities) are given?_____
   _____
   _____

3. What does this proverb teach me? _____
   _____
   _____
   _____
   _____

5 to 10 minutes.   Date _____

Proverb reference _____

1. What good traits (qualities) are given? _____

_____

_____

2. What bad traits (qualities) are given?_____

_____

_____

3. What does this proverb teach me? _____

_____

_____

_____

_____

5 to 10 minutes.   Date _____

Proverb reference _____

1. What good traits (qualities) are given? _____

_____

_____

2. What bad traits (qualities) are given?_____

_____

_____

3. What does this proverb teach me? _____

_____

_____

_____

_____

_____ 41

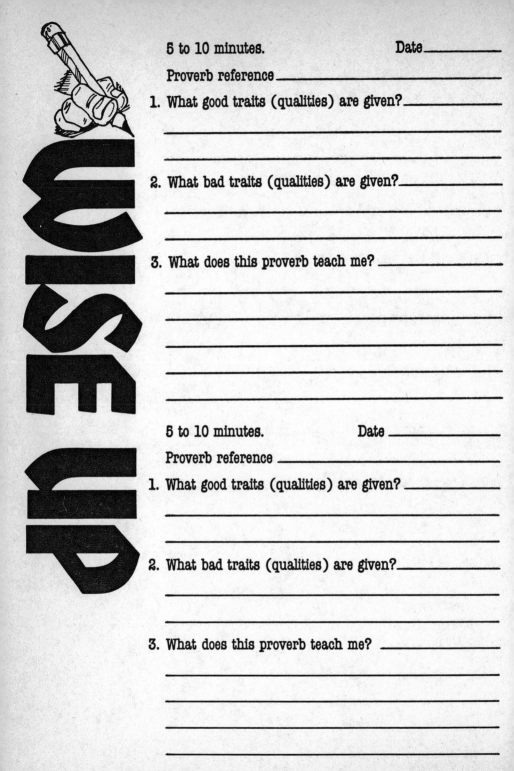

5 to 10 minutes.   Date_____

Proverb reference _____

1. What good traits (qualities) are given?_____
   _____
   _____

2. What bad traits (qualities) are given?_____
   _____
   _____

3. What does this proverb teach me? _____
   _____
   _____
   _____
   _____
   _____

5 to 10 minutes.   Date _____

Proverb reference _____

1. What good traits (qualities) are given? _____
   _____
   _____

2. What bad traits (qualities) are given?_____
   _____
   _____

3. What does this proverb teach me? _____
   _____
   _____
   _____
   _____

5 to 10 minutes.   Date _____

Proverb reference _____

1. What good traits (qualities) are given? _____

_____

_____

2. What bad traits (qualities) are given?_____

_____

_____

3. What does this proverb teach me? _____

_____

_____

_____

_____

5 to 10 minutes.   Date _____

Proverb reference _____

1. What good traits (qualities) are given? _____

_____

_____

2. What bad traits (qualities) are given?_____

_____

_____

3. What does this proverb teach me? _____

_____

_____

_____

_____

_____

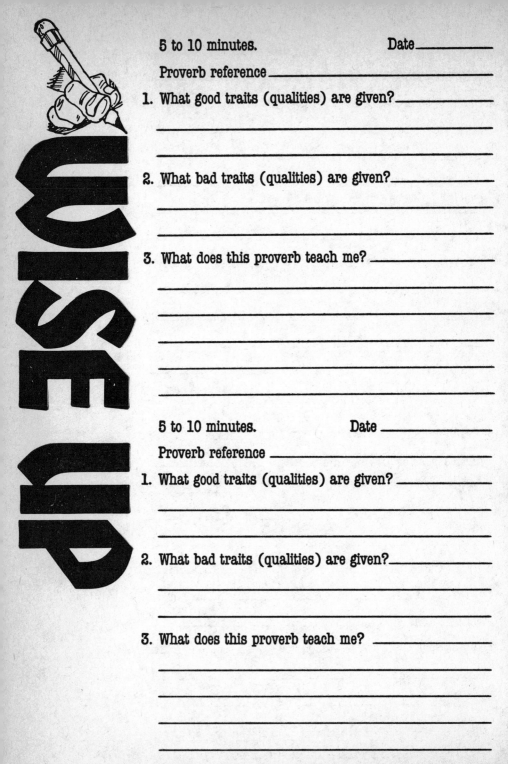

WISE UP

5 to 10 minutes.   Date _____

Proverb reference _____

1. What good traits (qualities) are given? _____
   _____
   _____

2. What bad traits (qualities) are given? _____
   _____
   _____

3. What does this proverb teach me? _____
   _____
   _____
   _____
   _____
   _____

5 to 10 minutes.   Date _____

Proverb reference _____

1. What good traits (qualities) are given? _____
   _____
   _____

2. What bad traits (qualities) are given? _____
   _____
   _____

3. What does this proverb teach me? _____
   _____
   _____
   _____
   _____
   _____

5 to 10 minutes.   Date _____

Proverb reference _____

1. What good traits (qualities) are given? _____

_____

_____

2. What bad traits (qualities) are given? _____

_____

_____

3. What does this proverb teach me? _____

_____

_____

_____

_____

5 to 10 minutes.   Date _____

Proverb reference _____

1. What good traits (qualities) are given? _____

_____

_____

2. What bad traits (qualities) are given? _____

_____

_____

3. What does this proverb teach me? _____

_____

_____

_____

_____

_____

WISE UP

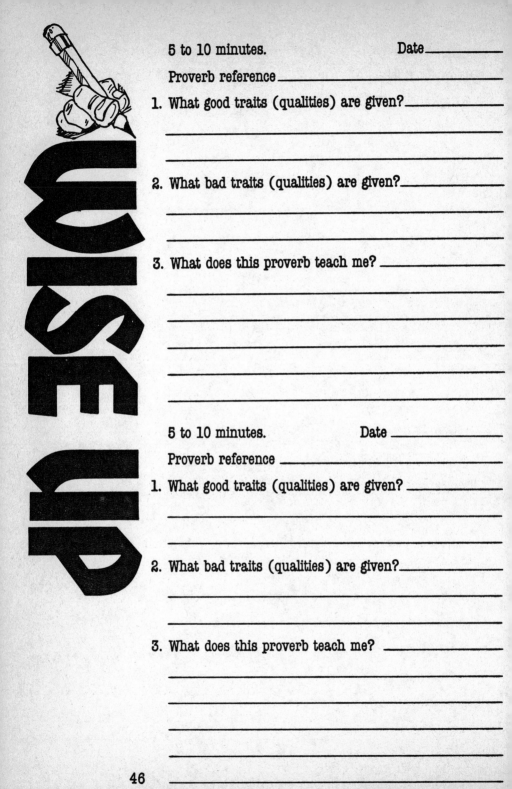

5 to 10 minutes.   Date _____

Proverb reference _____

1. What good traits (qualities) are given? _____
   _____
   _____

2. What bad traits (qualities) are given? _____
   _____
   _____

3. What does this proverb teach me? _____
   _____
   _____
   _____
   _____
   _____
   _____

5 to 10 minutes.   Date _____

Proverb reference _____

1. What good traits (qualities) are given? _____
   _____
   _____

2. What bad traits (qualities) are given? _____
   _____
   _____

3. What does this proverb teach me? _____
   _____
   _____
   _____

5 to 10 minutes.   Date _____

Proverb reference _____

1. What good traits (qualities) are given? _____

_____

_____

2. What bad traits (qualities) are given?_____

_____

_____

3. What does this proverb teach me? _____

_____

_____

_____

_____

5 to 10 minutes.   Date _____

Proverb reference _____

1. What good traits (qualities) are given? _____

_____

_____

2. What bad traits (qualities) are given?_____

_____

_____

3. What does this proverb teach me? _____

_____

_____

_____

_____

_____

WISE UP

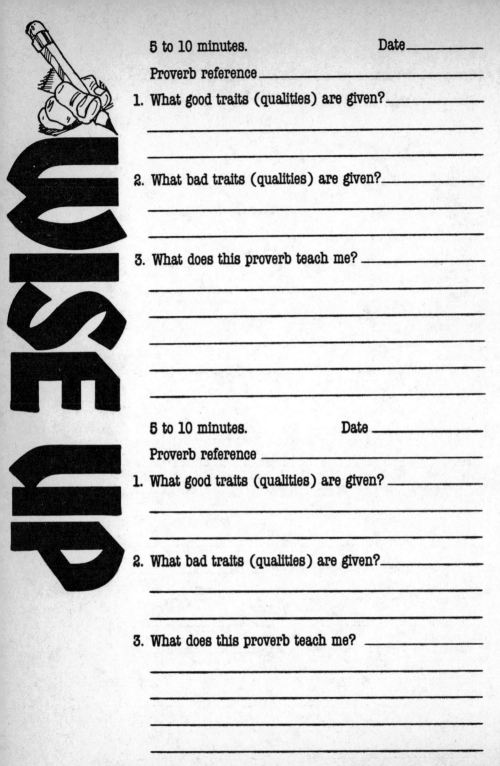

WISE UP

5 to 10 minutes.   Date_____

Proverb reference_____

1. What good traits (qualities) are given?_____
   _____
   _____

2. What bad traits (qualities) are given?_____
   _____
   _____

3. What does this proverb teach me? _____
   _____
   _____
   _____
   _____
   _____

5 to 10 minutes.   Date _____

Proverb reference _____

1. What good traits (qualities) are given? _____
   _____
   _____

2. What bad traits (qualities) are given?_____
   _____
   _____

3. What does this proverb teach me? _____
   _____
   _____
   _____
   _____

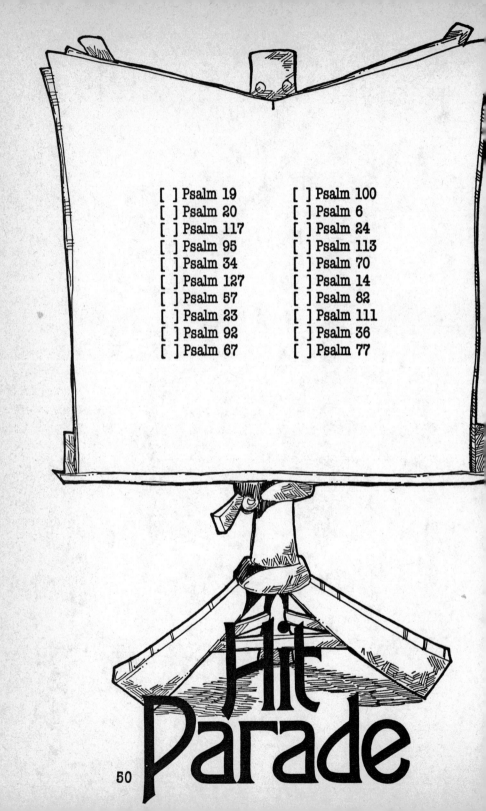

[ ] Psalm 19   [ ] Psalm 100
[ ] Psalm 20   [ ] Psalm 6
[ ] Psalm 117   [ ] Psalm 24
[ ] Psalm 95   [ ] Psalm 113
[ ] Psalm 34   [ ] Psalm 70
[ ] Psalm 127   [ ] Psalm 14
[ ] Psalm 57   [ ] Psalm 82
[ ] Psalm 23   [ ] Psalm 111
[ ] Psalm 92   [ ] Psalm 36
[ ] Psalm 67   [ ] Psalm 77

Hit
Parade

5 to 10 minutes.   Date _____

Psalm number _____

1. What does this Psalm talk about?

   [ ] A call for judgment   [ ] Praising God

   [ ] Sorrow over sin   [ ] Thanksgiving

   [ ] Prayer for help   [ ] Other _____

2. Copy the verse you like best: _____

   _____

   _____

   _____

3. What does this Psalm say to me? _____

   _____

   _____

   _____

5 to 10 minutes.   Date _____

Psalm number _____

1. What does this Psalm talk about?

   [ ] A call for judgment   [ ] Praising God

   [ ] Sorrow over sin   [ ] Thanksgiving

   [ ] Prayer for help   [ ] Other _____

2. Copy the verse you like best: _____

   _____

   _____

   _____

3. What does this Psalm say to me? _____

   _____

   _____

   _____

SING ALONG

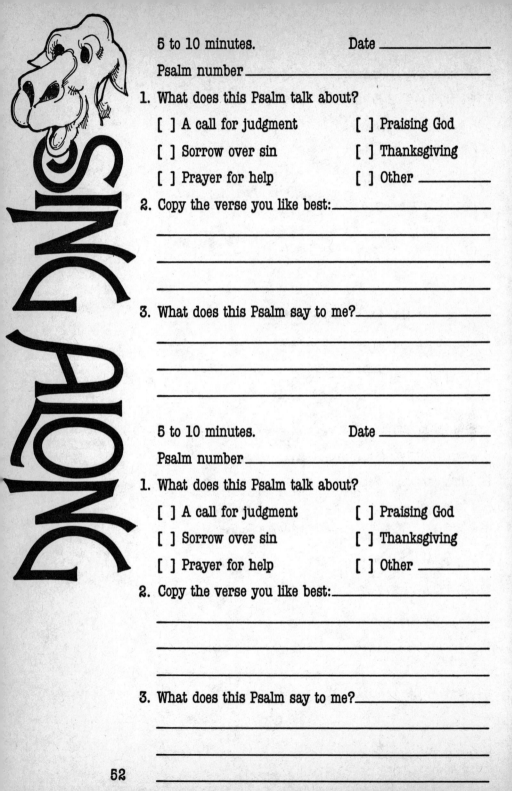

SING ALONG

5 to 10 minutes.   Date _____

Psalm number_____

1. What does this Psalm talk about?

   [ ] A call for judgment   [ ] Praising God

   [ ] Sorrow over sin   [ ] Thanksgiving

   [ ] Prayer for help   [ ] Other _____

2. Copy the verse you like best:_____

_____

_____

_____

3. What does this Psalm say to me?_____

_____

_____

_____

5 to 10 minutes.   Date _____

Psalm number_____

1. What does this Psalm talk about?

   [ ] A call for judgment   [ ] Praising God

   [ ] Sorrow over sin   [ ] Thanksgiving

   [ ] Prayer for help   [ ] Other _____

2. Copy the verse you like best:_____

_____

_____

_____

3. What does this Psalm say to me?_____

_____

_____

_____

5 to 10 minutes.   Date _____

Psalm number_____

1. What does this Psalm talk about?

   [ ] A call for judgment   [ ] Praising God

   [ ] Sorrow over sin   [ ] Thanksgiving

   [ ] Prayer for help   [ ] Other _____

2. Copy the verse you like best:_____

   _____

   _____

   _____

3. What does this Psalm say to me?_____

   _____

   _____

   _____

5 to 10 minutes.   Date _____

Psalm number_____

1. What does this Psalm talk about?

   [ ] A call for judgment   [ ] Praising God

   [ ] Sorrow over sin   [ ] Thanksgiving

   [ ] Prayer for help   [ ] Other _____

2. Copy the verse you like best:_____

   _____

   _____

   _____

3. What does this Psalm say to me?_____

   _____

   _____

   _____

SING ALONG

53

5 to 10 minutes.   Date _____

Psalm number_____

1. What does this Psalm talk about?

   [ ] A call for judgment   [ ] Praising God

   [ ] Sorrow over sin   [ ] Thanksgiving

   [ ] Prayer for help   [ ] Other _____

2. Copy the verse you like best:_____
   _____
   _____
   _____

3. What does this Psalm say to me?_____
   _____
   _____
   _____

5 to 10 minutes.   Date _____

Psalm number_____

1. What does this Psalm talk about?

   [ ] A call for judgment   [ ] Praising God

   [ ] Sorrow over sin   [ ] Thanksgiving

   [ ] Prayer for help   [ ] Other _____

2. Copy the verse you like best:_____
   _____
   _____
   _____

3. What does this Psalm say to me?_____
   _____
   _____

5 to 10 minutes.   Date _____

Psalm number _____

1. What does this Psalm talk about?

   [ ] A call for judgment   [ ] Praising God

   [ ] Sorrow over sin   [ ] Thanksgiving

   [ ] Prayer for help   [ ] Other _____

2. Copy the verse you like best: _____

_____

_____

_____

3. What does this Psalm say to me? _____

_____

_____

_____

5 to 10 minutes.   Date _____

Psalm number _____

1. What does this Psalm talk about?

   [ ] A call for judgment   [ ] Praising God

   [ ] Sorrow over sin   [ ] Thanksgiving

   [ ] Prayer for help   [ ] Other _____

2. Copy the verse you like best: _____

_____

_____

_____

3. What does this Psalm say to me? _____

_____

_____

_____

SING ALONG

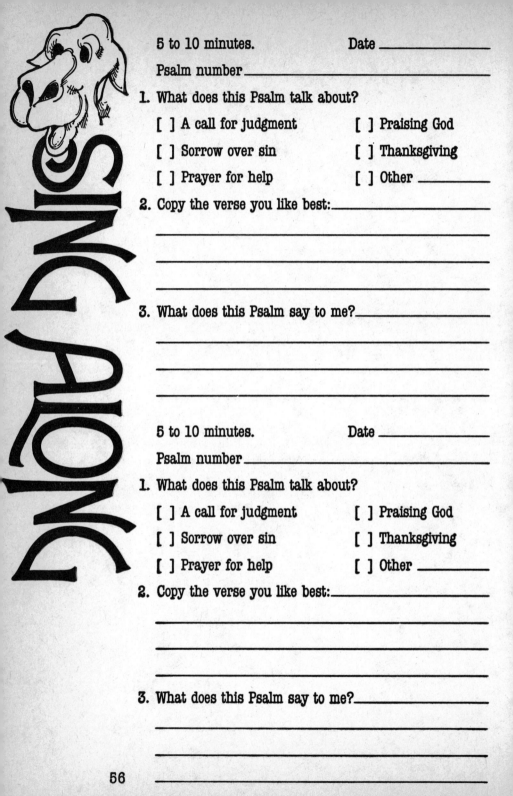

SING ALONG

5 to 10 minutes.   Date _____

Psalm number _____

1. What does this Psalm talk about?

    [ ] A call for judgment   [ ] Praising God

    [ ] Sorrow over sin   [ ] Thanksgiving

    [ ] Prayer for help   [ ] Other _____

2. Copy the verse you like best: _____

_____

_____

_____

3. What does this Psalm say to me? _____

_____

_____

_____

5 to 10 minutes.   Date _____

Psalm number _____

1. What does this Psalm talk about?

    [ ] A call for judgment   [ ] Praising God

    [ ] Sorrow over sin   [ ] Thanksgiving

    [ ] Prayer for help   [ ] Other _____

2. Copy the verse you like best: _____

_____

_____

_____

3. What does this Psalm say to me? _____

_____

_____

_____

5 to 10 minutes.   Date _____

Psalm number _____

. What does this Psalm talk about?

[ ] A call for judgment   [ ] Praising God

[ ] Sorrow over sin   [ ] Thanksgiving

[ ] Prayer for help   [ ] Other _____

. Copy the verse you like best: _____

_____

_____

_____

. What does this Psalm say to me? _____

_____

_____

_____

5 to 10 minutes.   Date _____

Psalm number _____

What does this Psalm talk about?

[ ] A call for judgment   [ ] Praising God

[ ] Sorrow over sin   [ ] Thanksgiving

[ ] Prayer for help   [ ] Other _____

. Copy the verse you like best: _____

_____

_____

_____

. What does this Psalm say to me? _____

_____

_____

_____

SING ALONG

SING ALONG

5 to 10 minutes.   Date _____

Psalm number _____

1. What does this Psalm talk about?

   [ ] A call for judgment   [ ] Praising God

   [ ] Sorrow over sin   [ ] Thanksgiving

   [ ] Prayer for help   [ ] Other _____

2. Copy the verse you like best: _____
   _____
   _____
   _____

3. What does this Psalm say to me? _____
   _____
   _____
   _____

5 to 10 minutes.   Date _____

Psalm number _____

1. What does this Psalm talk about?

   [ ] A call for judgment   [ ] Praising God

   [ ] Sorrow over sin   [ ] Thanksgiving

   [ ] Prayer for help   [ ] Other _____

2. Copy the verse you like best: _____
   _____
   _____
   _____

3. What does this Psalm say to me? _____
   _____
   _____

5 to 10 minutes.   Date _____

Psalm number _____

1. What does this Psalm talk about?

   [ ] A call for judgment   [ ] Praising God

   [ ] Sorrow over sin   [ ] Thanksgiving

   [ ] Prayer for help   [ ] Other _____

2. Copy the verse you like best: _____

   _____

   _____

   _____

3. What does this Psalm say to me? _____

   _____

   _____

   _____

5 to 10 minutes.   Date _____

Psalm number _____

1. What does this Psalm talk about?

   [ ] A call for judgment   [ ] Praising God

   [ ] Sorrow over sin   [ ] Thanksgiving

   [ ] Prayer for help   [ ] Other _____

2. Copy the verse you like best: _____

   _____

   _____

   _____

3. What does this Psalm say to me? _____

   _____

   _____

   _____

SING ALONG

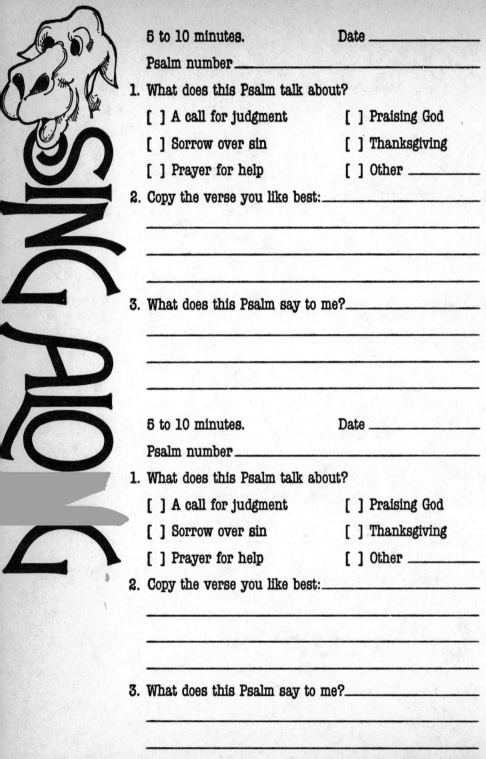

SING ALONG

5 to 10 minutes.   Date _____

Psalm number_____

1. What does this Psalm talk about?

[ ] A call for judgment   [ ] Praising God

[ ] Sorrow over sin   [ ] Thanksgiving

[ ] Prayer for help   [ ] Other _____

2. Copy the verse you like best:_____

_____

_____

_____

3. What does this Psalm say to me?_____

_____

_____

_____

5 to 10 minutes.   Date _____

Psalm number_____

1. What does this Psalm talk about?

[ ] A call for judgment   [ ] Praising God

[ ] Sorrow over sin   [ ] Thanksgiving

[ ] Prayer for help   [ ] Other _____

2. Copy the verse you like best:_____

_____

_____

_____

3. What does this Psalm say to me?_____

_____

_____

THE NAVIGATOR

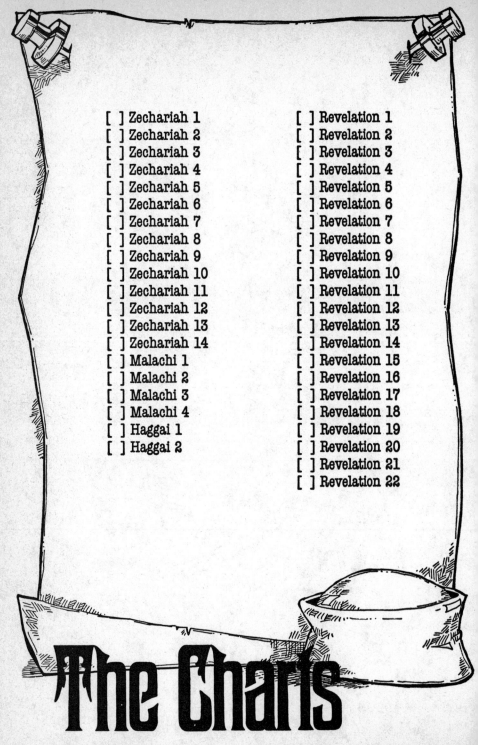

The Charts

5 to 10 minutes.

Prophecy Book _____

Put the passage references in the left hand column.
Tell what each chapter says in the summary column.
(If the chapter has more than one subject, you may
want to divide it into several paragraphs on the chart
below.) Put a "P" in the right hand column if the
passage predicts something.

Reference   Summary

_____

_____

_____

_____

_____

_____

_____

_____

_____

_____

_____

_____

_____

_____

_____

THE NAVIGATOR

THE NAVIGATOR

Reference	Summary

5 to 10 minutes.

Prophecy Book ————————————

Put the passage references in the left hand column.
Tell what each chapter says in the summary column.
(If the chapter has more than one subject, you may
want to divide it into several paragraphs on the chart
below.) Put a "P" in the right hand column if the
passage predicts something.

Reference   Summary

_____

_____

_____

_____

_____

_____

_____

_____

_____

_____

_____

_____

_____

_____

_____

_____

_____

_____

_____

_____

_____

_____

_____

THE NAVIGATOR

Reference	Summary

5 to 10 minutes.
Prophecy Book _____
Put the passage references in the left hand column.
Tell what each chapter says in the summary column.
(If the chapter has more than one subject, you may
want to divide it into several paragraphs on the chart
below.) Put a "P" in the right hand column if the
passage predicts something.

Reference	Summary

THE NAVIGATOR

Reference	Summary

5 to 10 minutes.

Prophecy Book _____

Put the passage references in the left hand column.
Tell what each chapter says in the summary column.
(If the chapter has more than one subject, you may
want to divide it into several paragraphs on the chart
below.) Put a "P" in the right hand column if the
passage predicts something.

Reference   Summary
_____

_____

_____

_____

_____

_____

_____

_____

_____

_____

_____

_____

_____

_____

_____

_____

_____

_____

_____

_____

THE NAVIGATOR

Reference   Summary

THE SURVEYOR

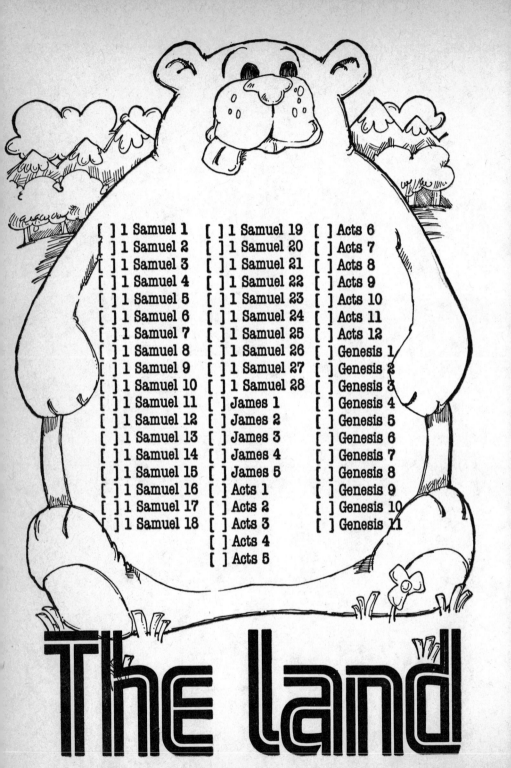

[ ] 1 Samuel 1   [ ] 1 Samuel 19   [ ] Acts 6
[ ] 1 Samuel 2   [ ] 1 Samuel 20   [ ] Acts 7
[ ] 1 Samuel 3   [ ] 1 Samuel 21   [ ] Acts 8
[ ] 1 Samuel 4   [ ] 1 Samuel 22   [ ] Acts 9
[ ] 1 Samuel 5   [ ] 1 Samuel 23   [ ] Acts 10
[ ] 1 Samuel 6   [ ] 1 Samuel 24   [ ] Acts 11
[ ] 1 Samuel 7   [ ] 1 Samuel 25   [ ] Acts 12
[ ] 1 Samuel 8   [ ] 1 Samuel 26   [ ] Genesis 1
[ ] 1 Samuel 9   [ ] 1 Samuel 27   [ ] Genesis 2
[ ] 1 Samuel 10   [ ] 1 Samuel 28   [ ] Genesis 3
[ ] 1 Samuel 11   [ ] James 1   [ ] Genesis 4
[ ] 1 Samuel 12   [ ] James 2   [ ] Genesis 5
[ ] 1 Samuel 13   [ ] James 3   [ ] Genesis 6
[ ] 1 Samuel 14   [ ] James 4   [ ] Genesis 7
[ ] 1 Samuel 15   [ ] James 5   [ ] Genesis 8
[ ] 1 Samuel 16   [ ] Acts 1   [ ] Genesis 9
[ ] 1 Samuel 17   [ ] Acts 2   [ ] Genesis 10
[ ] 1 Samuel 18   [ ] Acts 3   [ ] Genesis 11
                [ ] Acts 4
                [ ] Acts 5

The Land

5 to 10 minutes.

Book _____

Put the passage references in the left hand column.
Tell what each passage says in the summary column.
(If the chapter has more than one subject, you might
want to divide it into several sections on the chart
below.)

Reference	Summary

THE SURVEYOR

THE SURVEYOR

Reference	Summary

5 to 10 minutes.
Book _____

Put the passage references in the left hand column.
Tell what each passage says in the summary column.
(If the chapter has more than one subject, you might
want to divide it into several sections on the chart
below.)

Reference   Summary
_____
_____
_____
_____
_____
_____
_____
_____
_____
_____
_____
_____
_____
_____
_____
_____
_____
_____
_____
_____
_____
_____
_____
_____

THE SURVEYOR

THE SURVEYOR

Reference   Summary

5 to 10 minutes.

Book _____

Put the passage references in the left hand column.
Tell what each passage says in the summary column.
(If the chapter has more than one subject, you might
want to divide it into several sections on the chart
below.)

Reference	Summary

THE SURVEYOR

THE SURVEYOR

Reference	Summary

5 to 10 minutes.

Book _____

Put the passage references in the left hand column.
Tell what each passage says in the summary column.
(If the chapter has more than one subject, you might
want to divide it into several sections on the chart
below.)

Reference	Summary

THE SURVEYOR

THE SURVEYOR

Reference Summary

THE WATCHMAN

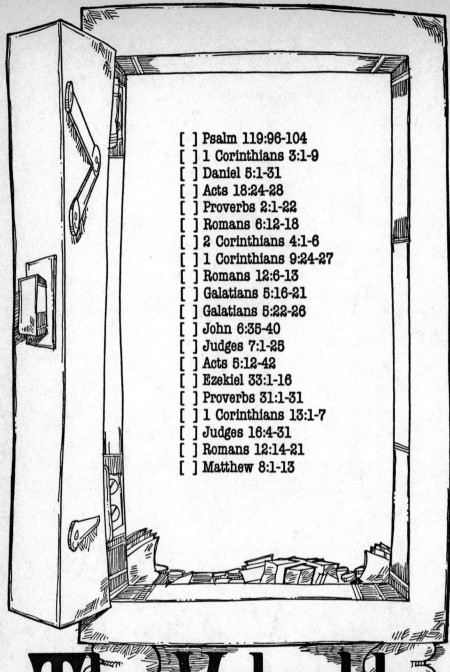

[ ] Psalm 119:96-104
[ ] 1 Corinthians 3:1-9
[ ] Daniel 5:1-31
[ ] Acts 18:24-28
[ ] Proverbs 2:1-22
[ ] Romans 6:12-18
[ ] 2 Corinthians 4:1-6
[ ] 1 Corinthians 9:24-27
[ ] Romans 12:6-13
[ ] Galatians 5:16-21
[ ] Galatians 5:22-26
[ ] John 6:35-40
[ ] Judges 7:1-25
[ ] Acts 5:12-42
[ ] Ezekiel 33:1-16
[ ] Proverbs 31:1-31
[ ] 1 Corinthians 13:1-7
[ ] Judges 16:4-31
[ ] Romans 12:14-21
[ ] Matthew 8:1-13

The Valuables

5 to 10 minutes.   Date _____

Passage _____
1. Read the passage, inspecting it carefully.
2. What did God teach me in this passage? _____
_____
_____
_____
_____

3. Copy the verse you want to think about today: _____
_____
_____
_____
_____

5 to 10 minutes.   Date _____

Passage _____
1. Read the passage, inspecting it carefully.
2. What did God teach me in this passage? _____
_____
_____
_____
_____

3. Copy the verse you want to think about today: _____
_____
_____
_____

THE WATCHMAN

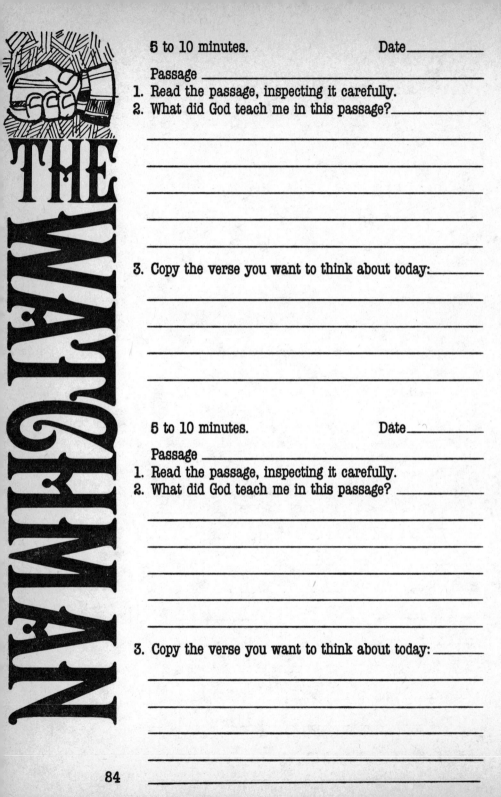

5 to 10 minutes. Date_____

Passage _____

1. Read the passage, inspecting it carefully.
2. What did God teach me in this passage?_____

_____

_____

_____

_____

_____

3. Copy the verse you want to think about today:_____

_____

_____

_____

_____

5 to 10 minutes. Date_____

Passage _____

1. Read the passage, inspecting it carefully.
2. What did God teach me in this passage? _____

_____

_____

_____

_____

_____

3. Copy the verse you want to think about today: _____

_____

_____

_____

_____

5 to 10 minutes.   Date _____

Passage _____

1. Read the passage, inspecting it carefully.
2. What did God teach me in this passage? _____

_____

_____

_____

_____

_____

3. Copy the verse you want to think about today: _____

_____

_____

_____

_____

5 to 10 minutes.   Date _____

Passage _____

1. Read the passage, inspecting it carefully.
2. What did God teach me in this passage? _____

_____

_____

_____

_____

3. Copy the verse you want to think about today: _____

_____

_____

_____

_____

THE WATCHMAN

5 to 10 minutes.   Date _____

Passage _____

1. Read the passage, inspecting it carefully.
2. What did God teach me in this passage? _____

_____

_____

_____

_____

_____

3. Copy the verse you want to think about today: _____

_____

_____

_____

_____

5 to 10 minutes.   Date _____

Passage _____

1. Read the passage, inspecting it carefully.
2. What did God teach me in this passage? _____

_____

_____

_____

_____

_____

3. Copy the verse you want to think about today: _____

_____

_____

_____

_____

5 to 10 minutes.   Date _____

Passage _____
1. Read the passage, inspecting it carefully.
2. What did God teach me in this passage? _____
_____
_____
_____
_____
_____

3. Copy the verse you want to think about today: _____
_____
_____
_____
_____

5 to 10 minutes.   Date _____

Passage _____
1. Read the passage, inspecting it carefully.
2. What did God teach me in this passage? _____
_____
_____
_____
_____
_____

3. Copy the verse you want to think about today: _____
_____
_____
_____
_____

THE WATCHMAN

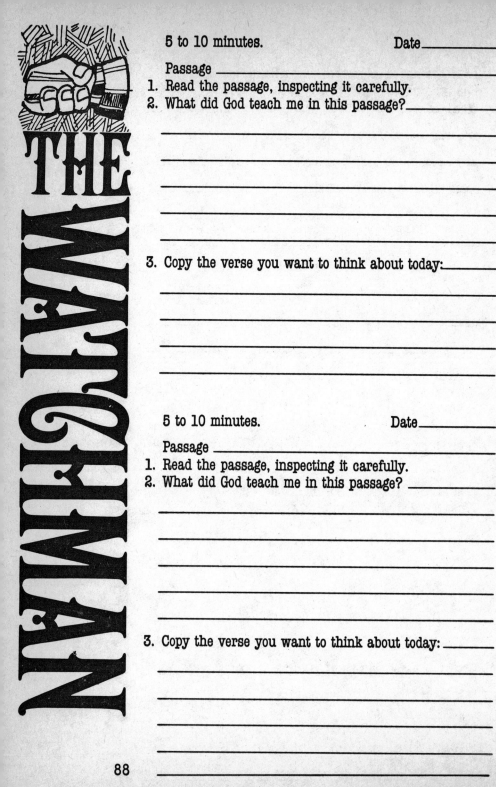

THE WATCHMAN

5 to 10 minutes.   Date_____

Passage _____

1. Read the passage, inspecting it carefully.
2. What did God teach me in this passage?_____
_____
_____
_____
_____
_____

3. Copy the verse you want to think about today:_____
_____
_____
_____
_____

5 to 10 minutes.   Date_____

Passage _____

1. Read the passage, inspecting it carefully.
2. What did God teach me in this passage? _____
_____
_____
_____
_____
_____

3. Copy the verse you want to think about today: _____
_____
_____
_____
_____

5 to 10 minutes.   Date _____

Passage _____
1. Read the passage, inspecting it carefully.
2. What did God teach me in this passage? _____

_____

_____

_____

_____

_____

3. Copy the verse you want to think about today: ____

_____

_____

_____

_____

5 to 10 minutes.   Date _____

Passage _____
1. Read the passage, inspecting it carefully.
2. What did God teach me in this passage? _____

_____

_____

_____

_____

_____

3. Copy the verse you want to think about today: ____

_____

_____

_____

_____

THE WATCHMAN

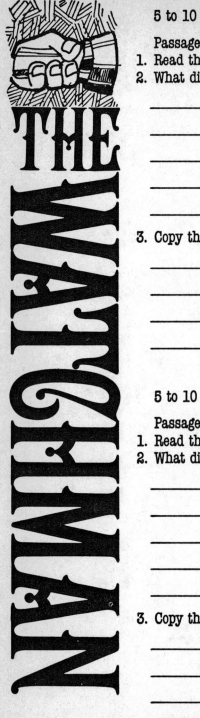

THE WATCHMAN

5 to 10 minutes.   Date_____

Passage _____

1. Read the passage, inspecting it carefully.
2. What did God teach me in this passage?_____

_____

_____

_____

_____

3. Copy the verse you want to think about today:_____

_____

_____

_____

_____

5 to 10 minutes.   Date_____

Passage _____

1. Read the passage, inspecting it carefully.
2. What did God teach me in this passage? _____

_____

_____

_____

_____

3. Copy the verse you want to think about today: _____

_____

_____

_____

_____

5 to 10 minutes.   Date _____

Passage _____
1. Read the passage, inspecting it carefully.
2. What did God teach me in this passage? _____
_____
_____
_____
_____
_____

3. Copy the verse you want to think about today: _____
_____
_____
_____
_____

5 to 10 minutes.   Date _____

Passage _____
1. Read the passage, inspecting it carefully.
2. What did God teach me in this passage? _____
_____
_____
_____
_____
_____

3. Copy the verse you want to think about today: _____
_____
_____
_____
_____

THE WAY GIVEN

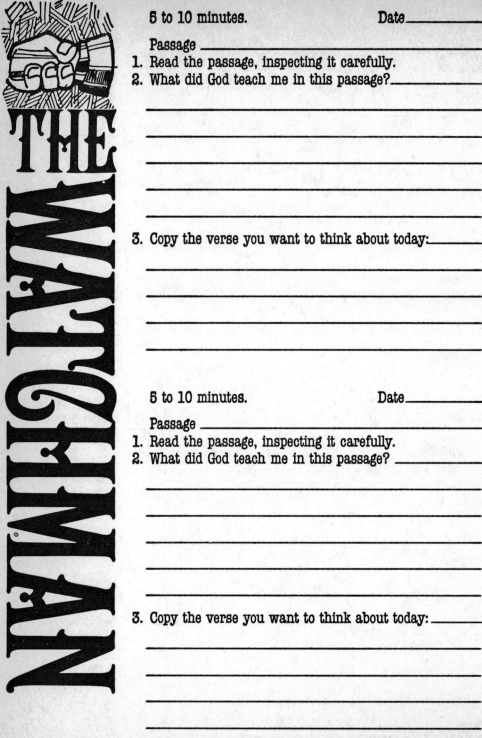

THE WATCHMAN

5 to 10 minutes.   Date_____

Passage _____
1. Read the passage, inspecting it carefully.
2. What did God teach me in this passage?_____
_____
_____
_____
_____
_____

3. Copy the verse you want to think about today:_____
_____
_____
_____
_____

5 to 10 minutes.   Date_____

Passage _____
1. Read the passage, inspecting it carefully.
2. What did God teach me in this passage? _____
_____
_____
_____
_____

3. Copy the verse you want to think about today: _____
_____
_____
_____
_____

MANHUNT

Wanted

Silas (Silvanus): Acts 15:22; Acts 16:16-40; 1 Pet. 5:12.

Eve: Gen. 2:21-25; 3:1-21.

Noah: Gen. 5:28-32; 6:8—9:1 9:28, 29.

Samson: Judg. 13:2—16:31.

Solomon: 2 Sam. 5:13-16; 1 Kgs. 2:12; 3:3-28; 5:1-5; 11:1-13; Prov. 1:1.

John the Baptist: Jn. 1:6, 7, 15-36; 3:23-30; Matt. 11:2-19; Mk. 6:14-29.

Philip: Acts 6:2-6; 8:4-13; 8:26-40; 21:7-9.

Ruth: Ruth 1—4.

Joseph: Gen. 30:22-24; 37:1-36; 39:1—45:28; 50:22-26.

15 to 20 minutes.   Date _____

Man You Are Hunting: _____

1. What he (she) did for a living: _____
_____

2. His background (family, ancestors, friends, when and where he lived): _____
_____
_____
_____
_____

3. A summary of his life: _____
_____
_____
_____
_____

4. Important events in his life: _____
_____
_____
_____
_____

5. His relationship with God: _____
_____
_____
_____

6. What can I learn from his life? _____
_____
_____
_____
_____

MANHUNT

15 to 20 minutes.   Date _____

Man You Are Hunting: _____

1. What he (she) did for a living: _____
   _____

2. His background (family, ancestors, friends, when and
   where he lived): _____
   _____
   _____
   _____
   _____

3. A summary of his life: _____
   _____
   _____
   _____
   _____

4. Important events in his life: _____
   _____
   _____
   _____
   _____

5. His relationship with God: _____
   _____
   _____
   _____

6. What can I learn from his life? _____
   _____
   _____
   _____
   _____

MANHUNT

15 to 20 minutes.   Date _____

Man You Are Hunting: _____

1. What he (she) did for a living: _____

   _____

2. His background (family, ancestors, friends, when and where he lived): _____

   _____

   _____

   _____

   _____

3. A summary of his life: _____

   _____

   _____

   _____

   _____

4. Important events in his life: _____

   _____

   _____

   _____

   _____

5. His relationship with God: _____

   _____

   _____

   _____

6. What can I learn from his life? _____

   _____

   _____

   _____

   _____

MANHUNT

15 to 20 minutes.   Date _____

Man You Are Hunting: _____

1. What he (she) did for a living: _____

2. His background (family, ancestors, friends, when and where he lived): _____
   _____
   _____
   _____
   _____

3. A summary of his life: _____
   _____
   _____
   _____

4. Important events in his life: _____
   _____
   _____
   _____
   _____

5. His relationship with God: _____
   _____
   _____
   _____

6. What can I learn from his life? _____
   _____
   _____
   _____

15 to 20 minutes.   Date _____

Man You Are Hunting: _____

1. What he (she) did for a living: _____
_____

2. His background (family, ancestors, friends, when and where he lived): _____
_____
_____
_____
_____

3. A summary of his life: _____
_____
_____
_____
_____

4. Important events in his life: _____
_____
_____
_____
_____

5. His relationship with God: _____
_____
_____
_____

6. What can I learn from his life? _____
_____
_____
_____
_____

MANHUNT

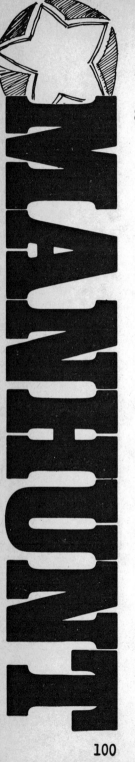

15 to 20 minutes.   Date _____

Man You Are Hunting: _____

1. What he (she) did for a living: _____
_____

2. His background (family, ancestors, friends, when and where he lived): _____
_____
_____
_____
_____

3. A summary of his life: _____
_____
_____
_____
_____

4. Important events in his life: _____
_____
_____
_____
_____

5. His relationship with God: _____
_____
_____
_____

6. What can I learn from his life? _____
_____
_____
_____
_____

15 to 20 minutes.   Date _____

Man You Are Hunting: _____

1. What he (she) did for a living: _____
_____

2. His background (family, ancestors, friends, when and
   where he lived): _____
_____
_____
_____
_____

3. A summary of his life: _____
_____
_____
_____
_____

4. Important events in his life: _____
_____
_____
_____
_____

5. His relationship with God: _____
_____
_____
_____
_____

6. What can I learn from his life? _____
_____
_____
_____
_____

MANHUNT

101

MANHUNT

15 to 20 minutes.   Date _____

Man You Are Hunting: _____

1. What he (she) did for a living: _____
   _____

2. His background (family, ancestors, friends, when and where he lived): _____
   _____
   _____
   _____
   _____
   _____

3. A summary of his life: _____
   _____
   _____
   _____
   _____
   _____

4. Important events in his life: _____
   _____
   _____
   _____
   _____
   _____

5. His relationship with God: _____
   _____
   _____
   _____
   _____

6. What can I learn from his life? _____
   _____
   _____
   _____
   _____

15 to 20 minutes.   Date _____

Man You Are Hunting: _____

1. What he (she) did for a living: _____
_____

2. His background (family, ancestors, friends, when and
   where he lived): _____
_____
_____
_____
_____

3. A summary of his life: _____
_____
_____
_____
_____

4. Important events in his life: _____
_____
_____
_____
_____

5. His relationship with God: _____
_____
_____
_____

6. What can I learn from his life? _____
_____
_____
_____
_____

MANHUNT

MANHUNT

15 to 20 minutes.   Date _____

Man You Are Hunting: _____

1. What he (she) did for a living: _____
_____

2. His background (family, ancestors, friends, when and where he lived): _____
_____
_____
_____
_____

3. A summary of his life: _____
_____
_____
_____
_____

4. Important events in his life: _____
_____
_____
_____
_____

5. His relationship with God: _____
_____
_____
_____

6. What can I learn from his life? _____
_____
_____
_____
_____

DAY IN COURT

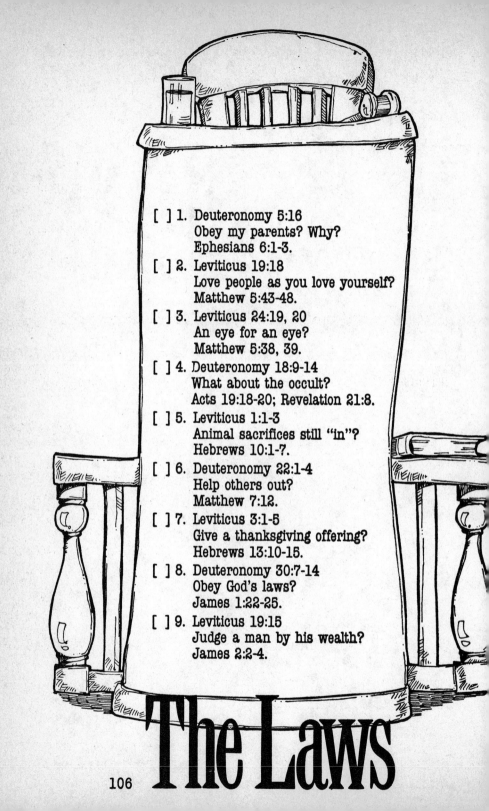

[ ] 1. Deuteronomy 5:16
Obey my parents? Why?
Ephesians 6:1-3.

[ ] 2. Leviticus 19:18
Love people as you love yourself?
Matthew 5:43-48.

[ ] 3. Leviticus 24:19, 20
An eye for an eye?
Matthew 5:38, 39.

[ ] 4. Deuteronomy 18:9-14
What about the occult?
Acts 19:18-20; Revelation 21:8.

[ ] 5. Leviticus 1:1-3
Animal sacrifices still "in"?
Hebrews 10:1-7.

[ ] 6. Deuteronomy 22:1-4
Help others out?
Matthew 7:12.

[ ] 7. Leviticus 3:1-5
Give a thanksgiving offering?
Hebrews 13:10-15.

[ ] 8. Deuteronomy 30:7-14
Obey God's laws?
James 1:22-25.

[ ] 9. Leviticus 19:15
Judge a man by his wealth?
James 2:2-4.

The Laws

15 to 20 minutes.   Date _____

Reference _____

1. What does this law command? _____
_____
_____
_____

2. Why do you think this law was given? _____
_____
_____
_____
_____

3. Has this law been done away in some other part of
   Scripture? (See second reference.) _____
_____
_____
_____

4. What does the New Testament teach on this
   principle? _____
_____
_____
_____
_____

5. What can I learn from this law? _____
_____
_____
_____
_____
_____

DAY IN COURT

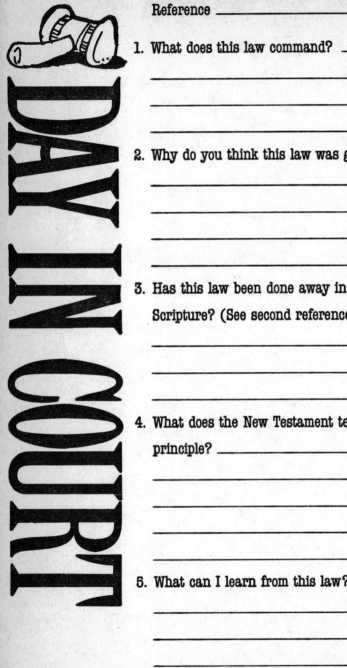

DAY IN COURT

15 to 20 minutes.   Date _____

Reference _____

1. What does this law command? _____
_____
_____
_____

2. Why do you think this law was given? _____
_____
_____
_____
_____

3. Has this law been done away in some other part of
Scripture? (See second reference.) _____
_____
_____
_____

4. What does the New Testament teach on this
principle? _____
_____
_____
_____
_____

5. What can I learn from this law? _____
_____
_____
_____
_____

15 to 20 minutes. Date _____

Reference _____

1. What does this law command? _____
_____
_____
_____

2. Why do you think this law was given? _____
_____
_____
_____
_____

3. Has this law been done away in some other part of Scripture? (See second reference.) _____
_____
_____
_____

4. What does the New Testament teach on this principle? _____
_____
_____
_____
_____

5. What can I learn from this law? _____
_____
_____
_____
_____
_____

DAY IN COURT

15 to 20 minutes.   Date _____

Reference _____

1. What does this law command? _____

_____

_____

_____

2. Why do you think this law was given? _____

_____

_____

_____

_____

3. Has this law been done away in some other part of
   Scripture? (See second reference.) _____

_____

_____

_____

4. What does the New Testament teach on this
   principle? _____

_____

_____

_____

_____

5. What can I learn from this law? _____

_____

_____

_____

_____

DAY IN COURT

15 to 20 minutes.   Date _____

Reference _____

1. What does this law command? _____
_____
_____
_____

2. Why do you think this law was given? _____
_____
_____
_____
_____

3. Has this law been done away in some other part of
Scripture? (See second reference.) _____
_____
_____
_____

4. What does the New Testament teach on this
principle? _____
_____
_____
_____
_____

5. What can I learn from this law? _____
_____
_____
_____
_____
_____

DAY IN COURT

15 to 20 minutes.   Date _____

Reference _____

DAY IN COURT

1. What does this law command? _____

_____

_____

_____

2. Why do you think this law was given? _____

_____

_____

_____

_____

3. Has this law been done away in some other part of
   Scripture? (See second reference.) _____

_____

_____

_____

4. What does the New Testament teach on this
   principle? _____

_____

_____

_____

_____

_____

5. What can I learn from this law? _____

_____

_____

_____

_____

15 to 20 minutes.   Date _____

Reference _____

1. What does this law command? _____

_____

_____

_____

2. Why do you think this law was given? _____

_____

_____

_____

3. Has this law been done away in some other part of

Scripture? (See second reference.) _____

_____

_____

_____

4. What does the New Testament teach on this

principle? _____

_____

_____

_____

5. What can I learn from this law? _____

_____

_____

_____

_____

DAY IN COURT

15 to 20 minutes.   Date _____

Reference _____

1. What does this law command? _____
   _____
   _____
   _____

2. Why do you think this law was given? _____
   _____
   _____
   _____
   _____

3. Has this law been done away in some other part of
   Scripture? (See second reference.) _____
   _____
   _____
   _____

4. What does the New Testament teach on this
   principle? _____
   _____
   _____
   _____
   _____

5. What can I learn from this law? _____
   _____
   _____
   _____
   _____

DAY IN COURT

15 to 20 minutes.   Date _____

Reference _____

1. What does this law command? _____
_____
_____
_____

2. Why do you think this law was given? _____
_____
_____
_____
_____

3. Has this law been done away in some other part of
Scripture? (See second reference.) _____
_____
_____

4. What does the New Testament teach on this
principle? _____
_____
_____
_____
_____

5. What can I learn from this law? _____
_____
_____
_____
_____

DAY IN COURT

15 to 20 minutes.   Date _____

Reference _____

DAY IN COURT

1. What does this law command? _____

   _____

   _____

   _____

2. Why do you think this law was given? _____

   _____

   _____

   _____

   _____

3. Has this law been done away in some other part of
   Scripture? (See second reference.) _____

   _____

   _____

   _____

4. What does the New Testament teach on this
   principle? _____

   _____

   _____

   _____

   _____

5. What can I learn from this law? _____

   _____

   _____

   _____

   _____

   _____

GET THAT STORY!

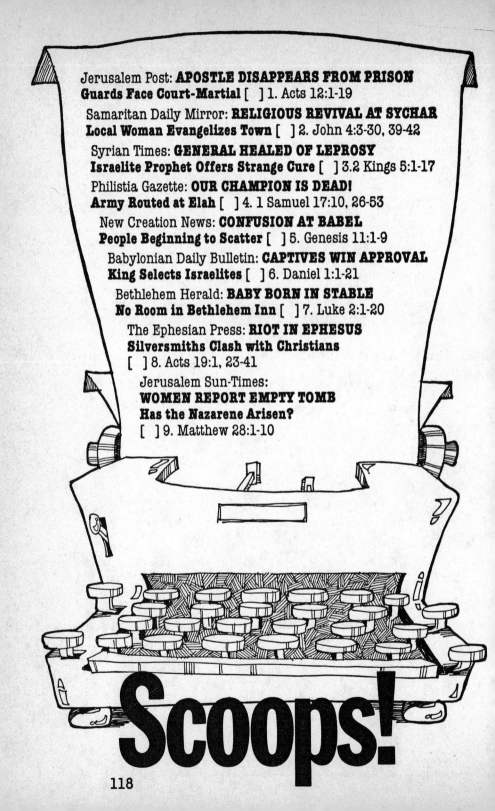

Jerusalem Post: **APOSTLE DISAPPEARS FROM PRISON**
Guards Face Court-Martial [ ] 1. Acts 12:1-19

Samaritan Daily Mirror: **RELIGIOUS REVIVAL AT SYCHAR**
Local Woman Evangelizes Town [ ] 2. John 4:3-30, 39-42

Syrian Times: **GENERAL HEALED OF LEPROSY**
Israelite Prophet Offers Strange Cure [ ] 3. 2 Kings 5:1-17

Philistia Gazette: **OUR CHAMPION IS DEAD!**
Army Routed at Elah [ ] 4. 1 Samuel 17:10, 26-53

New Creation News: **CONFUSION AT BABEL**
People Beginning to Scatter [ ] 5. Genesis 11:1-9

Babylonian Daily Bulletin: **CAPTIVES WIN APPROVAL**
King Selects Israelites [ ] 6. Daniel 1:1-21

Bethlehem Herald: **BABY BORN IN STABLE**
No Room in Bethlehem Inn [ ] 7. Luke 2:1-20

The Ephesian Press: **RIOT IN EPHESUS**
Silversmiths Clash with Christians
[ ] 8. Acts 19:1, 23-41

Jerusalem Sun-Times:
WOMEN REPORT EMPTY TOMB
Has the Nazarene Arisen?
[ ] 9. Matthew 28:1-10

Scoops!

15 to 20 minutes. Date _____

Passage selected: _____
Read the passage looking for all the things a
reporter looks for: who, when, where, what, and
why.

1. WHO is involved? _____
_____
_____

2. WHEN did this event take place? _____

   a. Is the day or hour given? _____

   b. What comes before or after this event? _____
     _____

3. WHERE did the action take place?

   a. Country, province, and city: _____
     _____

   b. Geography or landmarks: _____
     _____

   c. Other information: _____

4. WHAT took place? _____
_____
_____
_____

5. WHY did this event take place? _____
_____
_____

6. WHAT can I learn from this passage? _____
_____
_____

GET THAT STORY!

119

15 to 20 minutes.   Date _____

Passage selected: _____
Read the passage looking for all the things a
reporter looks for: who, when, where, what, and
why.

1. WHO is involved? _____

_____

_____

2. WHEN did this event take place? _____

   a. Is the day or hour given? _____

   b. What comes before or after this event? _____

_____

3. WHERE did the action take place?

   a. Country, province, and city: _____

_____

   b. Geography or landmarks: _____

_____

   c. Other information: _____

4. WHAT took place? _____

_____

_____

_____

5. WHY did this event take place? _____

_____

_____

6. WHAT can I learn from this passage? _____

_____

_____

15 to 20 minutes.   Date _____

Passage selected: _____
Read the passage looking for all the things a
reporter looks for: who, when, where, what, and
why.

1. WHO is involved? _____

_____

_____

2. WHEN did this event take place? _____

   a. Is the day or hour given? _____

   b. What comes before or after this event? _____

_____

3. WHERE did the action take place?

   a. Country, province, and city: _____

_____

   b. Geography or landmarks: _____

_____

   c. Other information: _____

4. WHAT took place? _____

_____

_____

_____

5. WHY did this event take place? _____

_____

_____

6. WHAT can I learn from this passage? _____

_____

_____

GET THAT STORY!

121

GET THAT STORY!

15 to 20 minutes.   Date _____

Passage selected: _____
Read the passage looking for all the things a
reporter looks for: who, when, where, what, and
why.

1. WHO is involved? _____

_____

_____

2. WHEN did this event take place? _____

 a. Is the day or hour given? _____

 b. What comes before or after this event? ____

_____

3. WHERE did the action take place?

 a. Country, province, and city: _____

_____

 b. Geography or landmarks: _____

_____

 c. Other information: _____

4. WHAT took place? _____

_____

_____

_____

5. WHY did this event take place? _____

_____

_____

6. WHAT can I learn from this passage? _____

_____

_____

122

15 to 20 minutes.   Date _____

Passage selected: _____
Read the passage looking for all the things a
reporter looks for: who, when, where, what, and
why.

1. WHO is involved? _____

_____

_____

2. WHEN did this event take place? _____

   a. Is the day or hour given? _____

   b. What comes before or after this event? _____

   _____

3. WHERE did the action take place?

   a. Country, province, and city: _____

   _____

   b. Geography or landmarks: _____

   _____

   c. Other information: _____

4. WHAT took place? _____

_____

_____

_____

5. WHY did this event take place? _____

_____

_____

6. WHAT can I learn from this passage? _____

_____

_____

GET THAT STORY!

123

15 to 20 minutes.   Date _____

Passage selected: _____
Read the passage looking for all the things a
reporter looks for: who, when, where, what, and
why.

1. WHO is involved? _____

   _____

   _____

2. WHEN did this event take place? _____

   a. Is the day or hour given? _____

   b. What comes before or after this event? ____

   _____

3. WHERE did the action take place?

   a. Country, province, and city: _____

   _____

   b. Geography or landmarks: _____

   _____

   c. Other information: _____

4. WHAT took place? _____

   _____

   _____

   _____

5. WHY did this event take place? _____

   _____

   _____

6. WHAT can I learn from this passage? ____

   _____

   _____

15 to 20 minutes.   Date _____

Passage selected: _____
Read the passage looking for all the things a
reporter looks for: who, when, where, what, and
why.

1. WHO is involved? _____

_____

_____

2. WHEN did this event take place? _____

   a. Is the day or hour given? _____

   b. What comes before or after this event? _____

   _____

3. WHERE did the action take place?

   a. Country, province, and city: _____

   _____

   b. Geography or landmarks: _____

   _____

   c. Other information: _____

4. WHAT took place? _____

_____

_____

_____

5. WHY did this event take place? _____

_____

_____

6. WHAT can I learn from this passage? _____

_____

_____

GET THAT STORY!

GET THAT STORY!

15 to 20 minutes.   Date _____

Passage selected: _____
Read the passage looking for all the things a
reporter looks for: who, when, where, what, and
why.

1. WHO is involved? _____
   _____
   _____

2. WHEN did this event take place? _____
   a. Is the day or hour given? _____
   b. What comes before or after this event? _____
      _____

3. WHERE did the action take place?
   a. Country, province, and city: _____
      _____
   b. Geography or landmarks: _____
      _____
   c. Other information: _____

4. WHAT took place? _____
   _____
   _____
   _____

5. WHY did this event take place? _____
   _____
   _____

6. WHAT can I learn from this passage? _____
   _____
   _____

15 to 20 minutes.   Date _____

Passage selected: _____
Read the passage looking for all the things a
reporter looks for: who, when, where, what, and
why.

1. WHO is involved? _____

_____

_____

2. WHEN did this event take place? _____

   a. Is the day or hour given? _____

   b. What comes before or after this event? _____

   _____

3. WHERE did the action take place?

   a. Country, province, and city: _____

   _____

   b. Geography or landmarks: _____

   _____

   c. Other information: _____

4. WHAT took place? _____

_____

_____

_____

5. WHY did this event take place? _____

_____

_____

6. WHAT can I learn from this passage? _____

_____

_____

GET THAT STORY!

15 to 20 minutes.   Date _____

Passage selected: _____
Read the passage looking for all the things a
reporter looks for: who, when, where, what, and
why.

1. WHO is involved? _____
   _____
   _____

2. WHEN did this event take place? _____
   a. Is the day or hour given? _____
   b. What comes before or after this event? _____
      _____

3. WHERE did the action take place?
   a. Country, province, and city: _____
      _____
   b. Geography or landmarks: _____
      _____
   c. Other information: _____

4. WHAT took place? _____
   _____
   _____
   _____

5. WHY did this event take place? _____
   _____
   _____

6. WHAT can I learn from this passage? _____
   _____
   _____

GET THAT STORY!

THE POSTAL INSPECTOR

[ ] 1. 2 Timothy 2:19-22
Dishes anyone?

[ ] 2. James 1:1-8
Don't try to
squirm out of it!

[ ] 3. Colossians 2:6-10
Do your roots
grow deep?

[ ] 4. Ephesians 4:17-24
Full of darkness
or light?

[ ] 5. 2 Corinthians 1:1-7
We're in trouble!

[ ] 6. Romans 8:5-9
What makes
a Christian?

[ ] 7. 2 Peter 1:1-7
How to get
God's peace.

[ ] 8. 2 John 5-11
Watch out for
false teachers!

[ ] 9. Philippians
1:20-24
Don't be caught
dead
without
Jesus!

Mail
Bag

15 to 20 minutes.   Date _____

Passage Selected _____

1. Does the author tell anything about himself or the people
   he's writing to? _____ What? _____
   _____
   _____

2. Was the author solving a problem? _____ If
   so, what was the problem? _____
   _____
   _____
   _____

3. Are we told not to do certain things? _____
   _____
   _____
   _____

4. What good things are we commanded to do? _____
   _____
   _____
   _____

5. What main thing does the passage teach? _____
   _____
   _____
   _____

6. What did God give me from this passage? _____
   _____
   _____
   _____

THE POSTAL INSPECTOR

THE POSTAL INSPECTOR

15 to 20 minutes.   Date _____

Passage Selected _____

1. Does the author tell anything about himself or the people he's writing to? _____ What? _____
_____
_____

2. Was the author solving a problem? _____ If so, what was the problem? _____
_____
_____
_____

3. Are we told not to do certain things? _____
_____
_____
_____

4. What good things are we commanded to do? _____
_____
_____
_____

5. What main thing does the passage teach? _____
_____
_____
_____

6. What did God give me from this passage? _____
_____
_____
_____

15 to 20 minutes.　　　　　Date _____

Passage Selected _____

1. Does the author tell anything about himself or the people
   he's writing to? _____ What? _____
   _____
   _____

2. Was the author solving a problem? _____ If
   so, what was the problem? _____
   _____
   _____
   _____

3. Are we told not to do certain things? _____
   _____
   _____
   _____

4. What good things are we commanded to do? _____
   _____
   _____
   _____

5. What main thing does the passage teach? _____
   _____
   _____

6. What did God give me from this passage? _____
   _____
   _____
   _____
   _____

THE POSTAL INSPECTOR

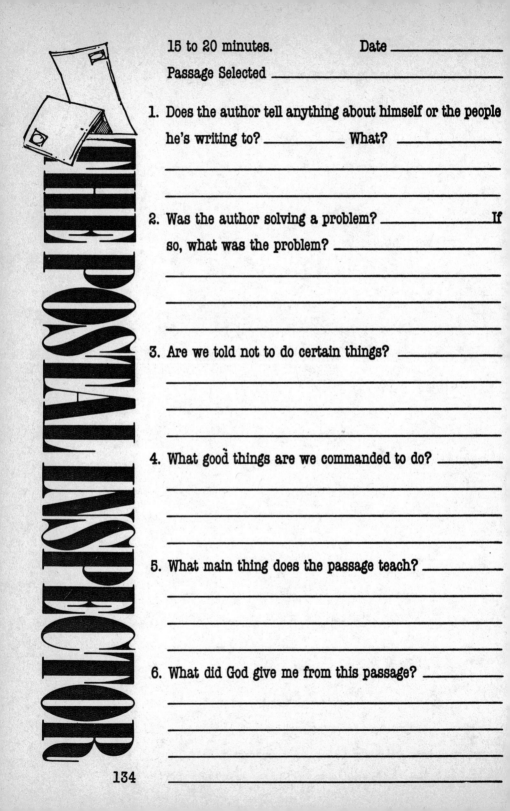

15 to 20 minutes.   Date _____

Passage Selected _____

1. Does the author tell anything about himself or the people he's writing to? _____ What? _____
_____
_____

2. Was the author solving a problem? _____ If so, what was the problem? _____
_____
_____
_____

3. Are we told not to do certain things? _____
_____
_____

4. What good things are we commanded to do? _____
_____
_____
_____

5. What main thing does the passage teach? _____
_____
_____
_____

6. What did God give me from this passage? _____
_____
_____

THE POSTAL INSPECTOR

15 to 20 minutes.   Date _____

Passage Selected _____

1. Does the author tell anything about himself or the people
   he's writing to? _____ What? _____
   _____
   _____

2. Was the author solving a problem? _____ If
   so, what was the problem? _____
   _____
   _____
   _____

3. Are we told not to do certain things? _____
   _____
   _____
   _____

4. What good things are we commanded to do? _____
   _____
   _____
   _____

5. What main thing does the passage teach? _____
   _____
   _____
   _____

6. What did God give me from this passage? _____
   _____
   _____
   _____

THE POSTAL INSPECTOR

THE POSTAL INSPECTOR

15 to 20 minutes.   Date _____

Passage Selected _____

1. Does the author tell anything about himself or the people he's writing to? _____ What? _____
   _____
   _____

2. Was the author solving a problem? _____ If so, what was the problem? _____
   _____
   _____
   _____

3. Are we told not to do certain things? _____
   _____
   _____
   _____

4. What good things are we commanded to do? _____
   _____
   _____
   _____

5. What main thing does the passage teach? _____
   _____
   _____
   _____

6. What did God give me from this passage? _____
   _____
   _____
   _____

15 to 20 minutes.   Date _____

Passage Selected _____

1. Does the author tell anything about himself or the people
he's writing to? _____ What? _____
_____
_____

2. Was the author solving a problem? _____ If
so, what was the problem? _____
_____
_____
_____

3. Are we told not to do certain things? _____
_____
_____
_____

4. What good things are we commanded to do? _____
_____
_____
_____

5. What main thing does the passage teach? _____
_____
_____
_____

6. What did God give me from this passage? _____
_____
_____
_____
_____

THE POSTAL INSPECTOR

137

15 to 20 minutes.   Date _____

Passage Selected _____

THE POSTAL INSPECTOR

1. Does the author tell anything about himself or the people he's writing to? _____ What? _____
   _____
   _____

2. Was the author solving a problem? _____ If so, what was the problem? _____
   _____
   _____
   _____

3. Are we told not to do certain things? _____
   _____
   _____
   _____

4. What good things are we commanded to do? _____
   _____
   _____
   _____

5. What main thing does the passage teach? _____
   _____
   _____
   _____

6. What did God give me from this passage? _____
   _____
   _____
   _____

15 to 20 minutes. Date _____

Passage Selected _____

1. Does the author tell anything about himself or the people he's writing to? _____ What? _____
_____
_____

2. Was the author solving a problem? _____ If so, what was the problem? _____
_____
_____
_____

3. Are we told not to do certain things? _____
_____
_____
_____

4. What good things are we commanded to do? _____
_____
_____
_____

5. What main thing does the passage teach? _____
_____
_____
_____

6. What did God give me from this passage? _____
_____
_____
_____

THE POSTAL INSPECTOR

THE POSTAL INSPECTOR

15 to 20 minutes.   Date _____

Passage Selected _____

1. Does the author tell anything about himself or the people he's writing to? _____ What? _____
_____
_____

2. Was the author solving a problem? _____ If so, what was the problem? _____
_____
_____
_____

3. Are we told not to do certain things? _____
_____
_____
_____

4. What good things are we commanded to do? _____
_____
_____
_____

5. What main thing does the passage teach? _____
_____
_____
_____

6. What did God give me from this passage? _____
_____
_____
_____
_____

THE FORECASTER

Forecasts

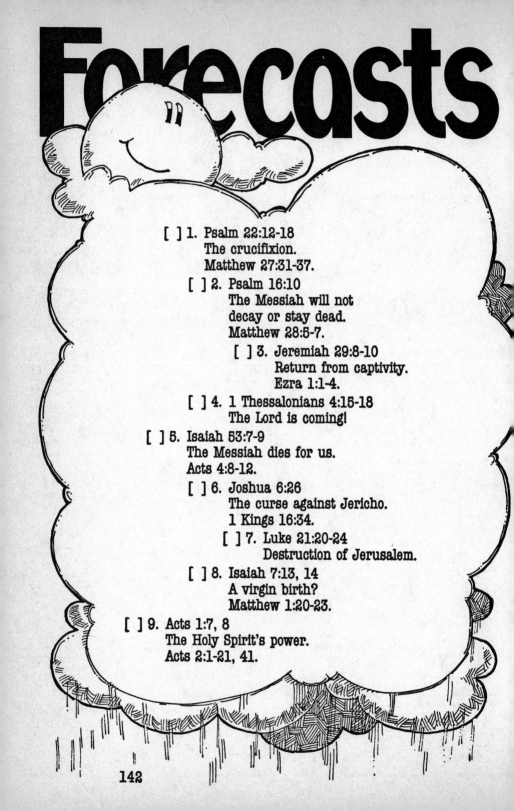

[ ] 1. Psalm 22:12-18
   The crucifixion.
   Matthew 27:31-37.

[ ] 2. Psalm 16:10
   The Messiah will not
   decay or stay dead.
   Matthew 28:5-7.

   [ ] 3. Jeremiah 29:8-10
      Return from captivity.
      Ezra 1:1-4.

[ ] 4. 1 Thessalonians 4:15-18
   The Lord is coming!

[ ] 5. Isaiah 53:7-9
   The Messiah dies for us.
   Acts 4:8-12.

   [ ] 6. Joshua 6:26
      The curse against Jericho.
      1 Kings 16:34.

      [ ] 7. Luke 21:20-24
         Destruction of Jerusalem.

   [ ] 8. Isaiah 7:13, 14
      A virgin birth?
      Matthew 1:20-23.

[ ] 9. Acts 1:7, 8
   The Holy Spirit's power.
   Acts 2:1-21, 41.

15 to 20 minutes. Date _____

Prophecy selected _____

1. What prophet is speaking? _____

_____

2. Can you tell who he is speaking to? _____

_____

3. Why was the prophecy given? _____

_____

_____

_____

4. What does the prophecy foretell? _____

_____

_____

_____

5. Has the prophecy been fulfilled? _____

_____

_____

_____

6. What can I learn from this prophecy? _____

_____

_____

_____

_____

_____

THE FORECASTER

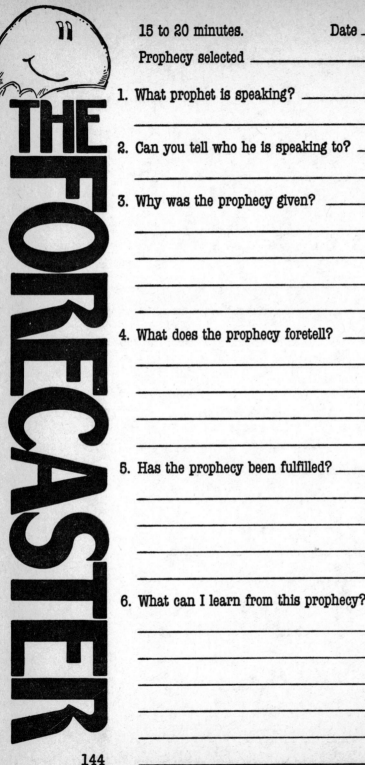

15 to 20 minutes.   Date _____

Prophecy selected _____

1. What prophet is speaking? _____
   _____

2. Can you tell who he is speaking to? _____
   _____

3. Why was the prophecy given? _____
   _____
   _____
   _____
   _____

4. What does the prophecy foretell? _____
   _____
   _____
   _____

5. Has the prophecy been fulfilled? _____
   _____
   _____
   _____

6. What can I learn from this prophecy? _____
   _____
   _____
   _____
   _____

15 to 20 minutes.   Date _____

Prophecy selected _____

THE FORECASTER

1. What prophet is speaking? _____
_____

2. Can you tell who he is speaking to? _____
_____

3. Why was the prophecy given? _____
_____
_____
_____

4. What does the prophecy foretell? _____
_____
_____
_____

5. Has the prophecy been fulfilled? _____
_____
_____
_____

6. What can I learn from this prophecy? _____
_____
_____
_____
_____

145

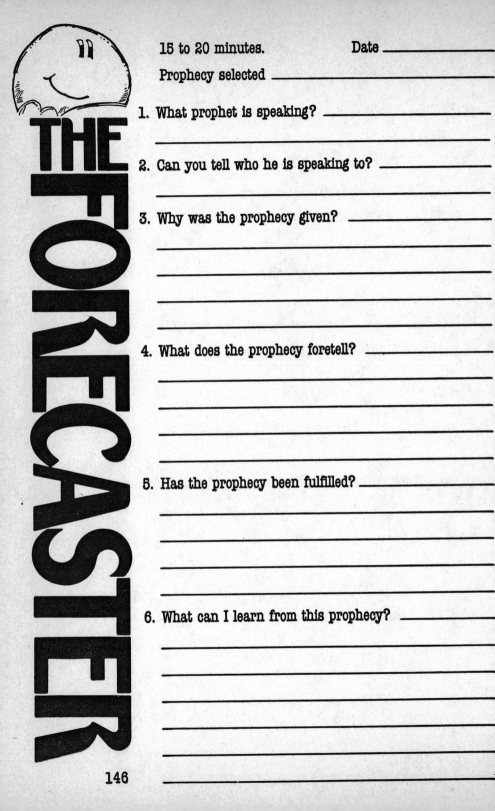

THE FORECASTER

15 to 20 minutes.   Date _____

Prophecy selected _____

1. What prophet is speaking? _____
   _____

2. Can you tell who he is speaking to? _____
   _____

3. Why was the prophecy given? _____
   _____
   _____
   _____
   _____

4. What does the prophecy foretell? _____
   _____
   _____
   _____
   _____

5. Has the prophecy been fulfilled? _____
   _____
   _____
   _____
   _____

6. What can I learn from this prophecy? _____
   _____
   _____
   _____
   _____
   _____

15 to 20 minutes.   Date _____

Prophecy selected _____

1. What prophet is speaking? _____
_____

2. Can you tell who he is speaking to? _____
_____

3. Why was the prophecy given? _____
_____
_____
_____
_____

4. What does the prophecy foretell? _____
_____
_____
_____
_____

5. Has the prophecy been fulfilled? _____
_____
_____
_____
_____

6. What can I learn from this prophecy? _____
_____
_____
_____
_____
_____

THE FORECASTER

147

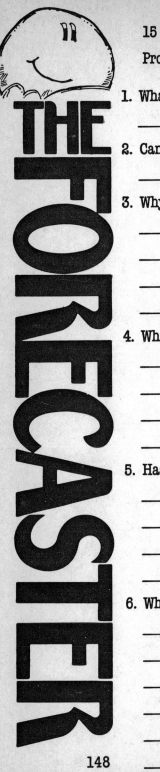

THE FORECASTER

15 to 20 minutes.   Date _____

Prophecy selected _____

1. What prophet is speaking? _____
   _____

2. Can you tell who he is speaking to? _____
   _____

3. Why was the prophecy given? _____
   _____
   _____
   _____
   _____

4. What does the prophecy foretell? _____
   _____
   _____
   _____
   _____

5. Has the prophecy been fulfilled? _____
   _____
   _____
   _____
   _____

6. What can I learn from this prophecy? _____
   _____
   _____
   _____
   _____
   _____

15 to 20 minutes.   Date _____

Prophecy selected _____

1. What prophet is speaking? _____
_____

2. Can you tell who he is speaking to? _____
_____

3. Why was the prophecy given? _____
_____
_____
_____
_____

4. What does the prophecy foretell? _____
_____
_____
_____
_____

5. Has the prophecy been fulfilled? _____
_____
_____
_____
_____

6. What can I learn from this prophecy? _____
_____
_____
_____
_____
_____

THE FORECASTER

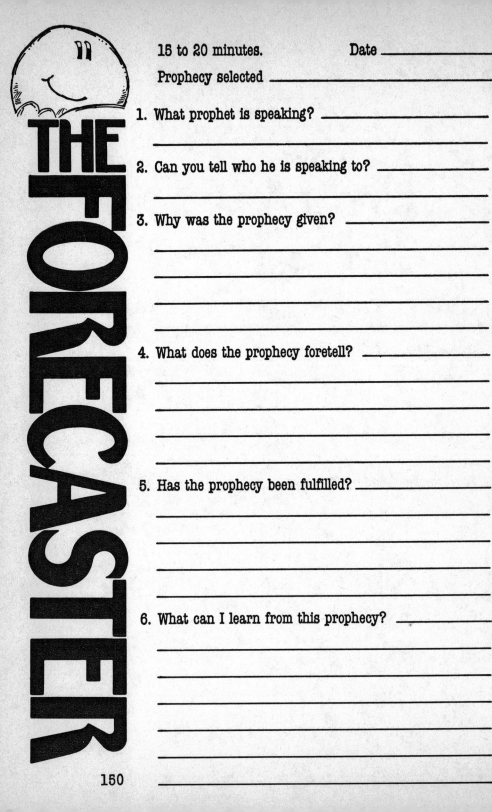

THE FORECASTER

15 to 20 minutes. Date _____

Prophecy selected _____

1. What prophet is speaking? _____
   _____

2. Can you tell who he is speaking to? _____
   _____

3. Why was the prophecy given? _____
   _____
   _____
   _____
   _____

4. What does the prophecy foretell? _____
   _____
   _____
   _____

5. Has the prophecy been fulfilled? _____
   _____
   _____
   _____
   _____

6. What can I learn from this prophecy? _____
   _____
   _____
   _____
   _____

15 to 20 minutes.   Date _____

Prophecy selected _____

1. What prophet is speaking? _____

_____

2. Can you tell who he is speaking to? _____

_____

3. Why was the prophecy given? _____

_____

_____

_____

_____

4. What does the prophecy foretell? _____

_____

_____

_____

_____

5. Has the prophecy been fulfilled? _____

_____

_____

_____

_____

6. What can I learn from this prophecy? _____

_____

_____

_____

_____

_____

THE FORECASTER

THE FORECASTER

15 to 20 minutes. Date _____

Prophecy selected _____

1. What prophet is speaking? _____
_____

2. Can you tell who he is speaking to? _____
_____

3. Why was the prophecy given? _____
_____
_____
_____
_____

4. What does the prophecy foretell? _____
_____
_____
_____
_____

5. Has the prophecy been fulfilled? _____
_____
_____
_____
_____

6. What can I learn from this prophecy? _____
_____
_____
_____
_____

THE UNIVERSITY

Great Lessons

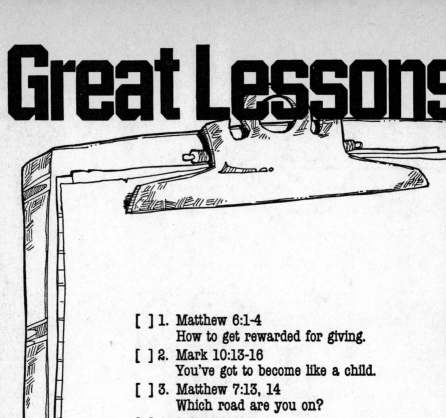

[ ] 1. Matthew 6:1-4
How to get rewarded for giving.

[ ] 2. Mark 10:13-16
You've got to become like a child.

[ ] 3. Matthew 7:13, 14
Which road are you on?

[ ] 4. Luke 9:23-25
What's the purpose of a cross?

[ ] 5. John 8:46-51
Who is this man?

[ ] 6. Mark 7:6-13
God's Word or tradition?

[ ] 7. Luke 12:1-5
Don't fear these hypocrites!

[ ] 8. Matthew 26:47-56
Swordplay in the garden.

[ ] 9. John 15:9-15
Live within My love.

15 to 20 minutes.   Date _____

Passage selected _____

1. What does Jesus condemn? _____

_____

Why? _____

_____

_____

2. What good qualities does He encourage? _____

_____

_____

_____

3. What things does Jesus discourage? _____

_____

_____

_____

4. What is the main thing He wants us to learn? ____

_____

_____

_____

5. Do I find it easy to do what Jesus says? _____

_____

_____

_____

6. How will this great lesson change my behavior? ___

_____

_____

_____

THE UNIVERSITY

THE UNIVERSITY

15 to 20 minutes.   Date _____

Passage selected _____

1. What does Jesus condemn? _____
_____

   Why? _____
_____
_____

2. What good qualities does He encourage? _____
_____
_____
_____

3. What things does Jesus discourage? _____
_____
_____
_____

4. What is the main thing He wants us to learn? ____
_____
_____
_____

5. Do I find it easy to do what Jesus says? _____
_____
_____
_____

6. How will this great lesson change my behavior? ___
_____
_____
_____
_____

15 to 20 minutes.   Date _____

Passage selected _____

1. What does Jesus condemn? _____
   _____

   Why? _____
   _____
   _____

2. What good qualities does He encourage? _____
   _____
   _____
   _____

3. What things does Jesus discourage? _____
   _____
   _____
   _____

4. What is the main thing He wants us to learn? _____
   _____
   _____
   _____

5. Do I find it easy to do what Jesus says? _____
   _____
   _____
   _____

6. How will this great lesson change my behavior? ___
   _____
   _____
   _____
   _____

THE UNIVERSITY

157

THE UNIVERSITY

15 to 20 minutes.   Date _____

Passage selected _____

1. What does Jesus condemn? _____
   _____

   Why? _____
   _____
   _____

2. What good qualities does He encourage? _____
   _____
   _____
   _____

3. What things does Jesus discourage? _____
   _____
   _____
   _____

4. What is the main thing He wants us to learn? _____
   _____
   _____
   _____

5. Do I find it easy to do what Jesus says? _____
   _____
   _____
   _____

6. How will this great lesson change my behavior? ____
   _____
   _____
   _____
   _____

15 to 20 minutes.   Date _____

Passage selected _____

1. What does Jesus condemn? _____
_____

Why? _____
_____
_____

2. What good qualities does He encourage? _____
_____
_____
_____

3. What things does Jesus discourage? _____
_____
_____
_____

4. What is the main thing He wants us to learn? ____
_____
_____
_____

5. Do I find it easy to do what Jesus says? _____
_____
_____
_____

6. How will this great lesson change my behavior? ___
_____
_____
_____

THE UNIVERSITY

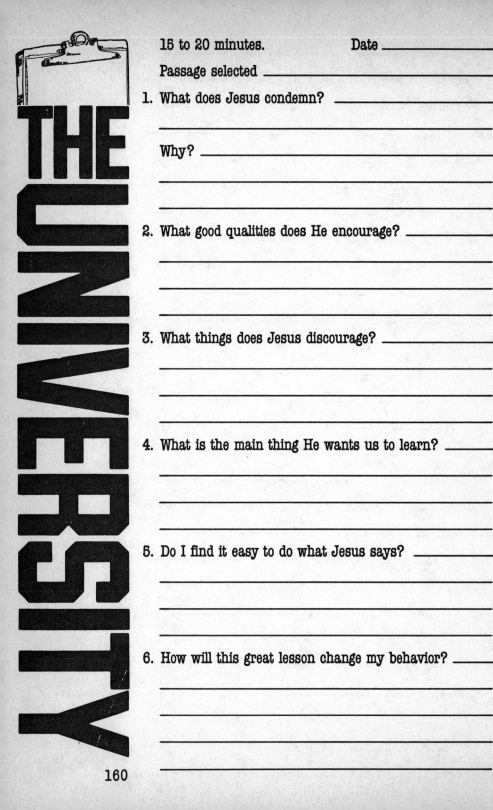

THE UNIVERSITY

15 to 20 minutes.   Date _____

Passage selected _____

1. What does Jesus condemn? _____
_____

   Why? _____
_____
_____

2. What good qualities does He encourage? _____
_____
_____
_____

3. What things does Jesus discourage? _____
_____
_____
_____

4. What is the main thing He wants us to learn? ____
_____
_____
_____

5. Do I find it easy to do what Jesus says? _____
_____
_____
_____

6. How will this great lesson change my behavior? ___
_____
_____
_____
_____

15 to 20 minutes.   Date _____

Passage selected _____

1. What does Jesus condemn? _____

_____

Why? _____

_____

_____

2. What good qualities does He encourage? _____

_____

_____

3. What things does Jesus discourage? _____

_____

_____

4. What is the main thing He wants us to learn? ___

_____

_____

_____

5. Do I find it easy to do what Jesus says? _____

_____

_____

6. How will this great lesson change my behavior? ___

_____

_____

_____

THE UNIVERSITY

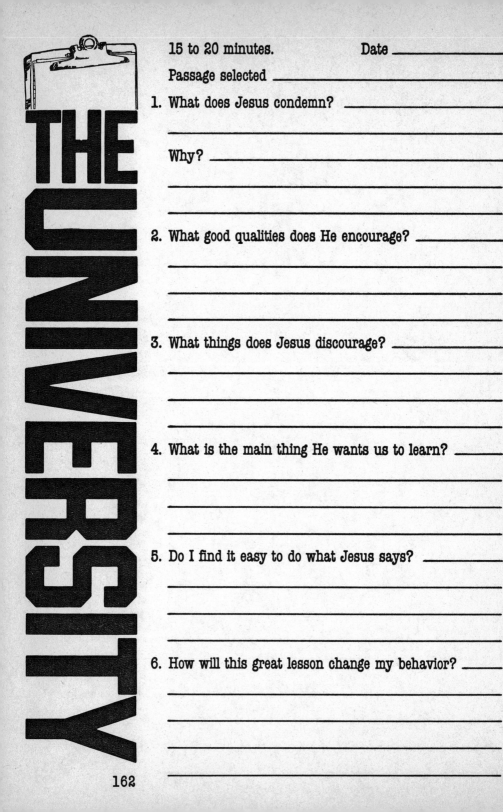

15 to 20 minutes.   Date _____

Passage selected _____

1. What does Jesus condemn? _____
   _____

   Why? _____
   _____
   _____

2. What good qualities does He encourage? _____
   _____
   _____
   _____

3. What things does Jesus discourage? _____
   _____
   _____
   _____

4. What is the main thing He wants us to learn? _____
   _____
   _____
   _____

5. Do I find it easy to do what Jesus says? _____
   _____
   _____
   _____

6. How will this great lesson change my behavior? ___
   _____
   _____
   _____

THE UNIVERSITY

15 to 20 minutes.   Date _____

Passage selected _____

1. What does Jesus condemn? _____
_____

Why? _____
_____
_____

2. What good qualities does He encourage? _____
_____
_____
_____

3. What things does Jesus discourage? _____
_____
_____
_____

4. What is the main thing He wants us to learn? _____
_____
_____
_____

5. Do I find it easy to do what Jesus says? _____
_____
_____
_____

6. How will this great lesson change my behavior? ____
_____
_____
_____
_____

THE UNIVERSITY

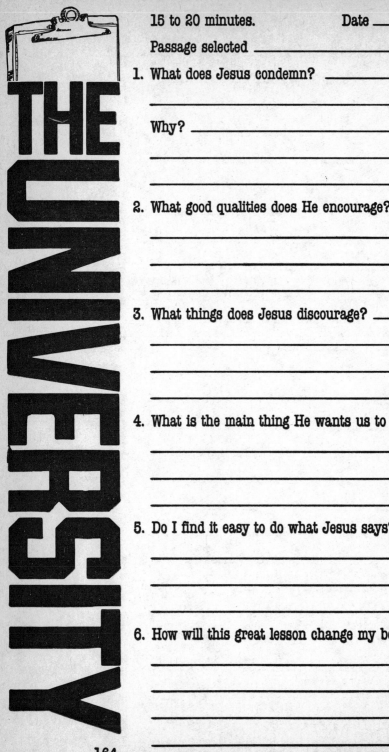

THE UNIVERSITY

15 to 20 minutes.   Date _____

Passage selected _____

1. What does Jesus condemn? _____
   _____

   Why? _____
   _____
   _____

2. What good qualities does He encourage? _____
   _____
   _____
   _____

3. What things does Jesus discourage? _____
   _____
   _____
   _____

4. What is the main thing He wants us to learn? ____
   _____
   _____
   _____

5. Do I find it easy to do what Jesus says? _____
   _____
   _____
   _____

6. How will this great lesson change my behavior? ___
   _____
   _____
   _____
   _____

164

STORY TIME

Best Sellers

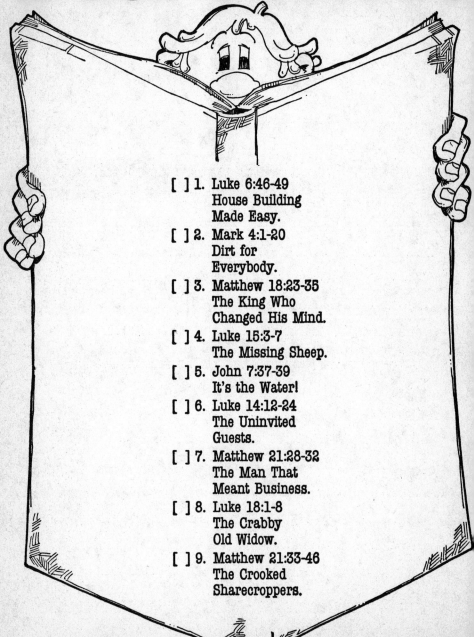

[ ] 1. Luke 6:46-49
House Building
Made Easy.

[ ] 2. Mark 4:1-20
Dirt for
Everybody.

[ ] 3. Matthew 18:23-35
The King Who
Changed His Mind.

[ ] 4. Luke 15:3-7
The Missing Sheep.

[ ] 5. John 7:37-39
It's the Water!

[ ] 6. Luke 14:12-24
The Uninvited
Guests.

[ ] 7. Matthew 21:28-32
The Man That
Meant Business.

[ ] 8. Luke 18:1-8
The Crabby
Old Widow.

[ ] 9. Matthew 21:33-46
The Crooked
Sharecroppers.

15 to 20 minutes.   Date _____

Passage Selected _____

1. What parable or story is told? _____
_____
_____

2. Briefly summarize the story: _____
_____
_____
_____

3. If Jesus gives the meaning, summarize it briefly: _____
_____
_____
_____

4. What is the main thing the story teaches? _____
_____
_____
_____

5. What extra spiritual truths are hidden in this
   parable? _____
_____
_____
_____
_____

6. How will this message change my behavior? _____
_____
_____
_____

167

15 to 20 minutes.   Date _____

Passage Selected _____

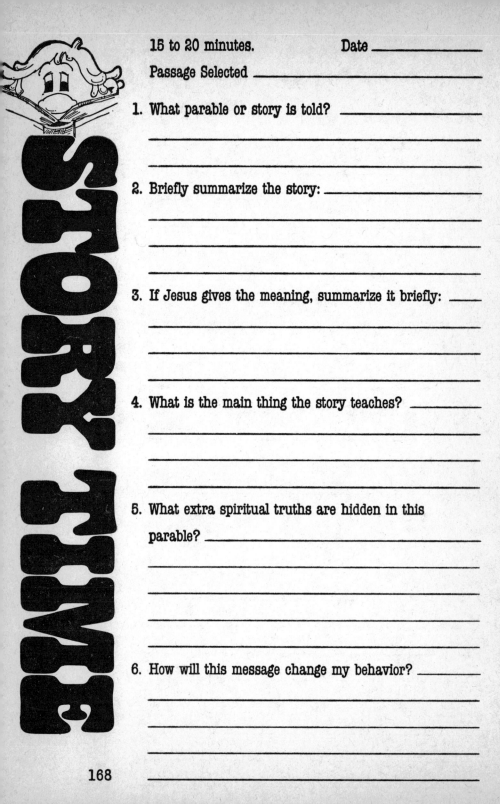

1. What parable or story is told? _____

_____

_____

2. Briefly summarize the story: _____

_____

_____

_____

3. If Jesus gives the meaning, summarize it briefly: ___

_____

_____

_____

4. What is the main thing the story teaches? _____

_____

_____

_____

5. What extra spiritual truths are hidden in this
   parable? _____

_____

_____

_____

_____

6. How will this message change my behavior? _____

_____

_____

_____

15 to 20 minutes.   Date _____

Passage Selected _____

1. What parable or story is told? _____
_____
_____

2. Briefly summarize the story: _____
_____
_____
_____

3. If Jesus gives the meaning, summarize it briefly: ____
_____
_____
_____

4. What is the main thing the story teaches? _____
_____
_____
_____

5. What extra spiritual truths are hidden in this
   parable? _____
_____
_____
_____
_____

6. How will this message change my behavior? _____
_____
_____
_____
_____

STORY TIME

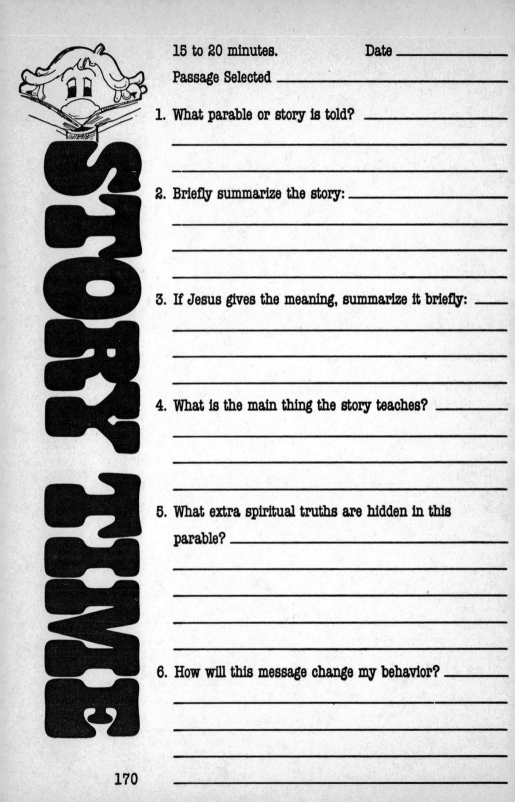

15 to 20 minutes.   Date _____

Passage Selected _____

1. What parable or story is told? _____

_____

_____

2. Briefly summarize the story: _____

_____

_____

_____

3. If Jesus gives the meaning, summarize it briefly: ___

_____

_____

_____

4. What is the main thing the story teaches? _____

_____

_____

_____

5. What extra spiritual truths are hidden in this

   parable? _____

_____

_____

_____

_____

6. How will this message change my behavior? _____

_____

_____

_____

_____

STORY TIME

15 to 20 minutes.   Date _____

Passage Selected _____

1. What parable or story is told? _____

_____

_____

2. Briefly summarize the story: _____

_____

_____

_____

3. If Jesus gives the meaning, summarize it briefly: ____

_____

_____

_____

4. What is the main thing the story teaches? _____

_____

_____

_____

5. What extra spiritual truths are hidden in this

   parable? _____

_____

_____

_____

_____

6. How will this message change my behavior? _____

_____

_____

_____

_____

STORY TIME

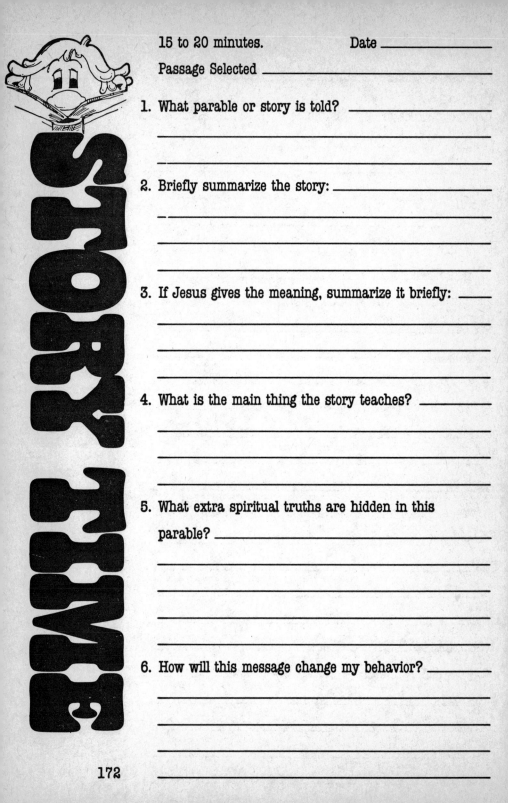

15 to 20 minutes.   Date _____

Passage Selected _____

1. What parable or story is told? _____
_____
_____

2. Briefly summarize the story: _____
_____
_____
_____

3. If Jesus gives the meaning, summarize it briefly: ____
_____
_____
_____

4. What is the main thing the story teaches? _____
_____
_____
_____

5. What extra spiritual truths are hidden in this
   parable? _____
_____
_____
_____
_____

6. How will this message change my behavior? _____
_____
_____
_____
_____

STORY TIME

15 to 20 minutes.   Date _____

Passage Selected _____

1. What parable or story is told? _____

_____

_____

2. Briefly summarize the story: _____

_____

_____

_____

3. If Jesus gives the meaning, summarize it briefly: ____

_____

_____

_____

4. What is the main thing the story teaches? _____

_____

_____

_____

5. What extra spiritual truths are hidden in this

   parable? _____

_____

_____

_____

_____

6. How will this message change my behavior? _____

_____

_____

_____

STORY TIME

173

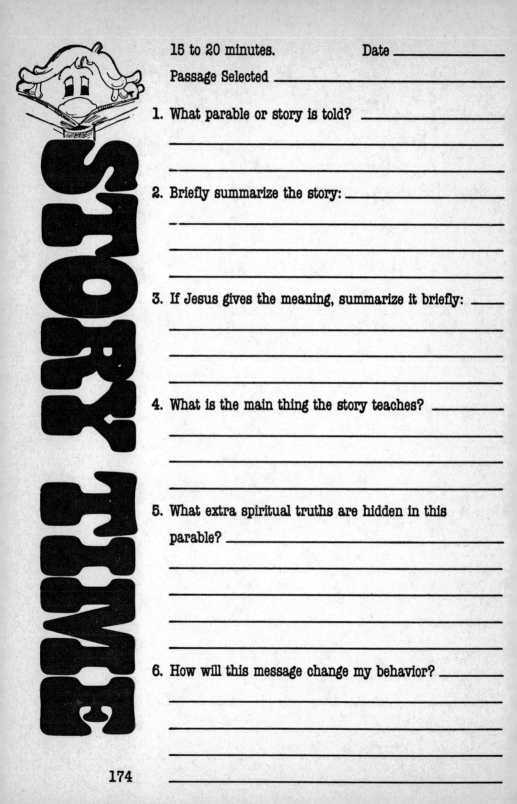

15 to 20 minutes.   Date _____

Passage Selected _____

1. What parable or story is told? _____
   _____
   _____

2. Briefly summarize the story: _____
   _____
   _____
   _____

3. If Jesus gives the meaning, summarize it briefly: ____
   _____
   _____
   _____

4. What is the main thing the story teaches? _____
   _____
   _____
   _____

5. What extra spiritual truths are hidden in this
   parable? _____
   _____
   _____
   _____
   _____

6. How will this message change my behavior? _____
   _____
   _____
   _____

STORY TIME

15 to 20 minutes.   Date _____

Passage Selected _____

1. What parable or story is told? _____
_____
_____

2. Briefly summarize the story: _____
_____
_____
_____

3. If Jesus gives the meaning, summarize it briefly: ___
_____
_____
_____

4. What is the main thing the story teaches? _____
_____
_____
_____

5. What extra spiritual truths are hidden in this

   parable? _____
_____
_____
_____

6. How will this message change my behavior? _____
_____
_____
_____

STORY TIME

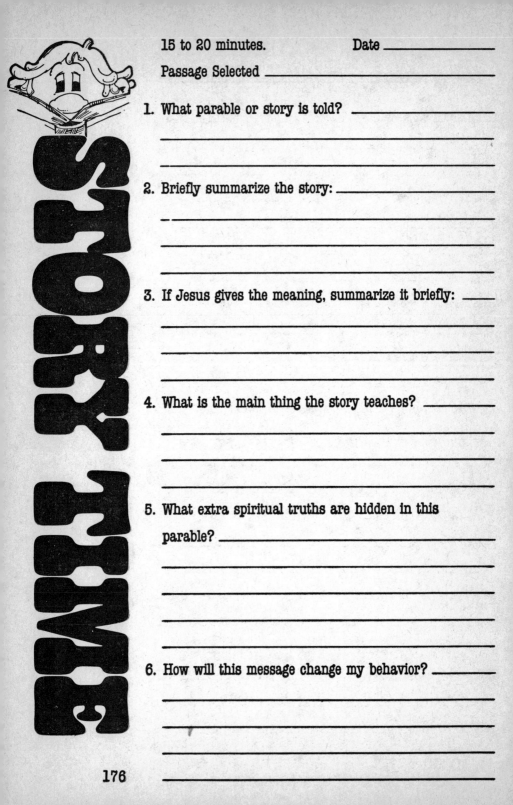

15 to 20 minutes.   Date _____

Passage Selected _____

1. What parable or story is told? _____
_____
_____

2. Briefly summarize the story: _____
_____
_____
_____

3. If Jesus gives the meaning, summarize it briefly: ____
_____
_____
_____

4. What is the main thing the story teaches? _____
_____
_____
_____

5. What extra spiritual truths are hidden in this
   parable? _____
_____
_____
_____

6. How will this message change my behavior? _____
_____
_____
_____

STORY TIME

THE
DETECTIVE

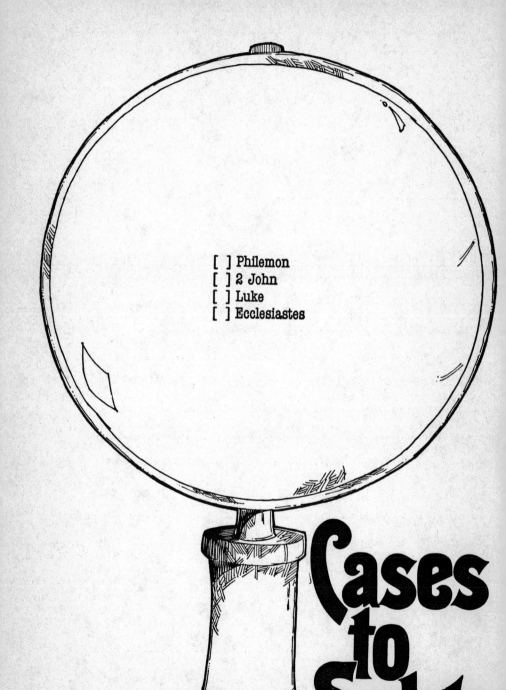

[ ] Philemon
[ ] 2 John
[ ] Luke
[ ] Ecclesiastes

Cases
to
Solve

20 to 30 minutes.   Date _____

Book Selected _____

1. Who is the writer? _____

2. Tell everything you know about the writer: _____
_____
_____
_____

3. Who was the book written to? _____
_____
_____

4. Why was the book written? _____
_____
_____

5. How many chapters does the book have? _____

6. What are some of the important teachings in the book?
_____
_____
_____
_____

7. Write out an important verse: _____
_____
_____
_____

8. What can I learn from this book? _____
_____
_____
_____

THE DETECTIVE

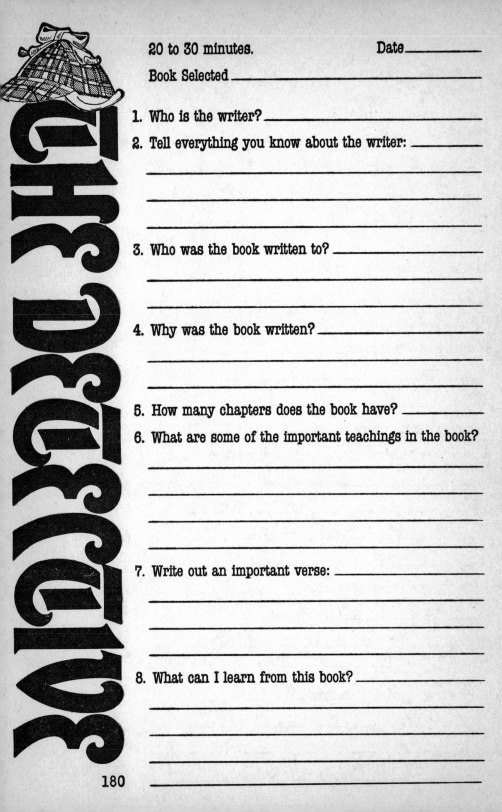

THE DETECTIVE

20 to 30 minutes.   Date_____

Book Selected _____

1. Who is the writer? _____

2. Tell everything you know about the writer: _____
_____
_____
_____

3. Who was the book written to? _____
_____
_____

4. Why was the book written? _____
_____
_____

5. How many chapters does the book have? _____

6. What are some of the important teachings in the book?
_____
_____
_____
_____

7. Write out an important verse: _____
_____
_____
_____

8. What can I learn from this book? _____
_____
_____
_____

20 to 30 minutes.   Date _____

Book Selected _____

1. Who is the writer? _____

2. Tell everything you know about the writer: _____
_____
_____
_____

3. Who was the book written to? _____
_____
_____

4. Why was the book written? _____
_____
_____

5. How many chapters does the book have? _____

6. What are some of the important teachings in the book?
_____
_____
_____
_____

7. Write out an important verse: _____
_____
_____
_____

8. What can I learn from this book? _____
_____
_____
_____ 181

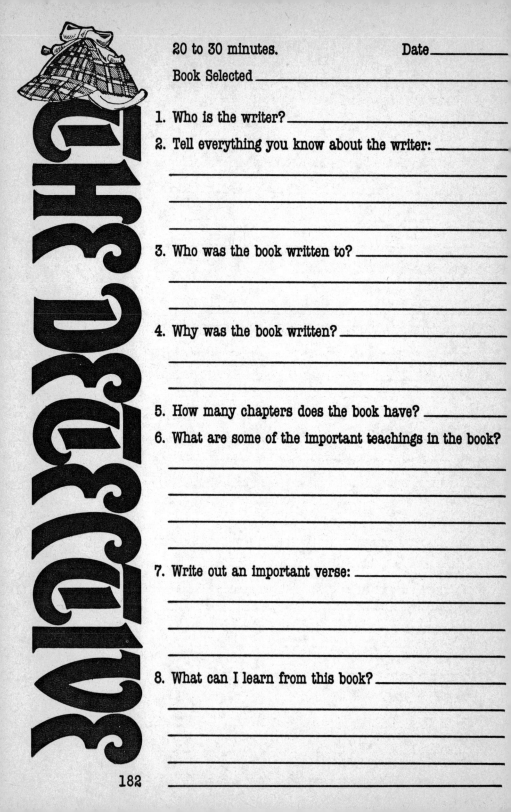

THE DETECTIVE

20 to 30 minutes.   Date_____

Book Selected _____

1. Who is the writer?_____

2. Tell everything you know about the writer: _____
   _____
   _____
   _____

3. Who was the book written to? _____
   _____
   _____

4. Why was the book written?_____
   _____
   _____

5. How many chapters does the book have? _____

6. What are some of the important teachings in the book?
   _____
   _____
   _____
   _____

7. Write out an important verse: _____
   _____
   _____
   _____

8. What can I learn from this book?_____
   _____
   _____
   _____

Use this Logbook to record the studies you do each day. Put the name of the method you use opposite the correct day and month. The Logbook will help you stay faithful in your promise to God.

Year _____

Month _____

Month _____

1. _____	1. _____
2. _____	2. _____
3. _____	3. _____
4. _____	4. _____
5. _____	5. _____
6. _____	6. _____
7. _____	7. _____
8. _____	8. _____
9. _____	9. _____
10. _____	10. _____
11. _____	11. _____
12. _____	12. _____
13. _____	13. _____
14. _____	14. _____
15. _____	15. _____
16. _____	16. _____
17. _____	17. _____
18. _____	18. _____
19. _____	19. _____
20. _____	20. _____
21. _____	21. _____
22. _____	22. _____
23. _____	23. _____
24. _____	24. _____
25. _____	25. _____
26. _____	26. _____
27. _____	27. _____
28. _____	28. _____
29. _____	29. _____
30. _____	30. _____
31. _____	31. _____

LOGBOOK

Year _____

Month _____

Month _____

Use this Logbook to record the studies you do each day. Put the name of the method you use opposite the correct day and month. The Logbook will help you stay faithful in your promise to God.

LOGBOOK

1. _____
2. _____
3. _____
4. _____
5. _____
6. _____
7. _____
8. _____
9. _____
10. _____
11. _____
12. _____
13. _____
14. _____
15. _____
16. _____
17. _____
18. _____
19. _____
20. _____
21. _____
22. _____
23. _____
24. _____
25. _____
26. _____
27. _____
28. _____
29. _____
30. _____
31. _____

1. _____
2. _____
3. _____
4. _____
5. _____
6. _____
7. _____
8. _____
9. _____
10. _____
11. _____
12. _____
13. _____
14. _____
15. _____
16. _____
17. _____
18. _____
19. _____
20. _____
21. _____
22. _____
23. _____
24. _____
25. _____
26. _____
27. _____
28. _____
29. _____
30. _____
31. _____

Use this Logbook to record the studies you do each day. Put the name of the method you use opposite the correct day and month. The Logbook will help you stay faithful in your promise to God.

Year _____

Month _____

Month _____

1. _____	1. _____
2. _____	2. _____
3. _____	3. _____
4. _____	4. _____
5. _____	5. _____
6. _____	6. _____
7. _____	7. _____
8. _____	8. _____
9. _____	9. _____
10. _____	10. _____
11. _____	11. _____
12. _____	12. _____
13. _____	13. _____
14. _____	14. _____
15. _____	15. _____
16. _____	16. _____
17. _____	17. _____
18. _____	18. _____
19. _____	19. _____
20. _____	20. _____
21. _____	21. _____
22. _____	22. _____
23. _____	23. _____
24. _____	24. _____
25. _____	25. _____
26. _____	26. _____
27. _____	27. _____
28. _____	28. _____
29. _____	29. _____
30. _____	30. _____
31. _____	31. _____

LOGBOOK

Year _____

Month _____

Month _____

Use this Logbook to record the studies you do each day. Put the name of the method you use opposite the correct day and month. The Logbook will help you stay faithful in your promise to God.

LOGBOOK

1. _____	1. _____
2. _____	2. _____
3. _____	3. _____
4. _____	4. _____
5. _____	5. _____
6. _____	6. _____
7. _____	7. _____
8. _____	8. _____
9. _____	9. _____
10. _____	10. _____
11. _____	11. _____
12. _____	12. _____
13. _____	13. _____
14. _____	14. _____
15. _____	15. _____
16. _____	16. _____
17. _____	17. _____
18. _____	18. _____
19. _____	19. _____
20. _____	20. _____
21. _____	21. _____
22. _____	22. _____
23. _____	23. _____
24. _____	24. _____
25. _____	25. _____
26. _____	26. _____
27. _____	27. _____
28. _____	28. _____
29. _____	29. _____
30. _____	30. _____
31. _____	31. _____

Use this Logbook to record the studies you do each day. Put the name of the method you use opposite the correct day and month. The Logbook will help you stay faithful in your promise to God.

Year _____
Month _____
Month _____

#		#	
1.	_____	1.	_____
2.	_____	2.	_____
3.	_____	3.	_____
4.	_____	4.	_____
5.	_____	5.	_____
6.	_____	6.	_____
7.	_____	7.	_____
8.	_____	8.	_____
9.	_____	9.	_____
10.	_____	10.	_____
11.	_____	11.	_____
12.	_____	12.	_____
13.	_____	13.	_____
14.	_____	14.	_____
15.	_____	15.	_____
16.	_____	16.	_____
17.	_____	17.	_____
18.	_____	18.	_____
19.	_____	19.	_____
20.	_____	20.	_____
21.	_____	21.	_____
22.	_____	22.	_____
23.	_____	23.	_____
24.	_____	24.	_____
25.	_____	25.	_____
26.	_____	26.	_____
27.	_____	27.	_____
28.	_____	28.	_____
29.	_____	29.	_____
30.	_____	30.	_____
31.	_____	31.	_____

LOGBOOK

Year _____

Month _____

Month _____

Use this Logbook to record the studies you do each day. Put the name of the method you use opposite the correct day and month. The Logbook will help you stay faithful in your promise to God.

LOGBOOK

1. _____	1. _____
2. _____	2. _____
3. _____	3. _____
4. _____	4. _____
5. _____	5. _____
6. _____	6. _____
7. _____	7. _____
8. _____	8. _____
9. _____	9. _____
10. _____	10. _____
11. _____	11. _____
12. _____	12. _____
13. _____	13. _____
14. _____	14. _____
15. _____	15. _____
16. _____	16. _____
17. _____	17. _____
18. _____	18. _____
19. _____	19. _____
20. _____	20. _____
21. _____	21. _____
22. _____	22. _____
23. _____	23. _____
24. _____	24. _____
25. _____	25. _____
26. _____	26. _____
27. _____	27. _____
28. _____	28. _____
29. _____	29. _____
30. _____	30. _____
31. _____	31. _____

Use this Logbook to record the studies you do each day. Put the name of the method you use opposite the correct day and month. The Logbook will help you stay faithful in your promise to God.

Year _____

Month _____

Month _____

1. _____	1. _____
2. _____	2. _____
3. _____	3. _____
4. _____	4. _____
5. _____	5. _____
6. _____	6. _____
7. _____	7. _____
8. _____	8. _____
9. _____	9. _____
10. _____	10. _____
11. _____	11. _____
12. _____	12. _____
13. _____	13. _____
14. _____	14. _____
15. _____	15. _____
16. _____	16. _____
17. _____	17. _____
18. _____	18. _____
19. _____	19. _____
20. _____	20. _____
21. _____	21. _____
22. _____	22. _____
23. _____	23. _____
24. _____	24. _____
25. _____	25. _____
26. _____	26. _____
27. _____	27. _____
28. _____	28. _____
29. _____	29. _____
30. _____	30. _____
31. _____	31. _____

LOGBOOK

Year _____

Month _____

Month _____

Use this Logbook to record the studies you do each day. Put the name of the method you use opposite the correct day and month. The Logbook will help you stay faithful in your promise to God.

LOGBOOK

1. _____	1. _____
2. _____	2. _____
3. _____	3. _____
4. _____	4. _____
5. _____	5. _____
6. _____	6. _____
7. _____	7. _____
8. _____	8. _____
9. _____	9. _____
10. _____	10. _____
11. _____	11. _____
12. _____	12. _____
13. _____	13. _____
14. _____	14. _____
15. _____	15. _____
16. _____	16. _____
17. _____	17. _____
18. _____	18. _____
19. _____	19. _____
20. _____	20. _____
21. _____	21. _____
22. _____	22. _____
23. _____	23. _____
24. _____	24. _____
25. _____	25. _____
26. _____	26. _____
27. _____	27. _____
28. _____	28. _____
29. _____	29. _____
30. _____	30. _____
31. _____	31. _____